For my grandparents, Emil and Anna Busch, for exemplifying the values of clear thinking and hard work.

Arthur Whimbey

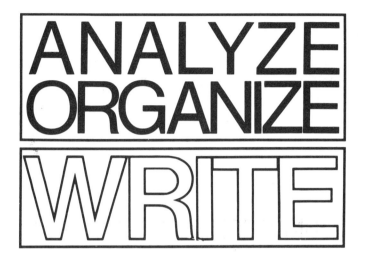

ANALYZE ORGANIZE WRITE

a structured program for expository writing

REVISED EDITION

Arthur Whimbey
Elizabeth Lynn Jenkins

 LAWRENCE ERLBAUM ASSOCIATES, PUBLISHERS

1987   Hillsdale, New Jersey   London

The Cover design, representing the contribution that verbalizing can make to thinking, is based on a remark from an Apopka High School student who was using the text *Problem Solving and Comprehension* (1986, Lawrence Erlbaum Associates):

> Thinking aloud problem solving helps me to look carefully at all of the parts of the problem, just like looking through a magnifying glass. Then I can fit all the facts and ideas into whole relationships.

Writing extends this precision that speech brings to thought.

Lawrence Erlbaum Associates, Inc., Publishers
365 Broadway
Hillsdale, New Jersey 07642

Library of Congress Cataloging-in-Publication Data

Whimbey, Arthur.
    Analyze, organize, write.

1. English language — Composition and exercises —
Problems, exercises, etc. 2. Exposition (Rhetoric) —
Problems, exercises, etc. I. Jenkins, Elizabeth Lynn.
II. Title.
PE1408.W577   1987   808'.042'076   87-9032
ISBN 0-8058-0082-4

Printed in the United States of America
20 19 18 17 16 15 14 13

Table of Contents

Preface To Students

Most professional writers agree that the surest way to become a better writer is to read, think, and write a great deal. *Analyze, Organize, Write* is an intensive program in doing this. Many of the exercises present you with a set of jumbled sentences which are like pieces of a puzzle that can be arranged into a complete picture. You will read the sentences and analyze the ideas to see how each piece fits together with the other pieces to form a coherent description or argument. Then you will write the sentences (from memory as much as possible) in the best logical order to form a convincing, informative paper. In some units you will be asked to organize and write sentences for several such papers before beginning your own, original papers. Do not think this is a waste of time. These exercises give you firsthand experience with a variety of ideas as well as sentence and argument patterns that you can employ in your own writing. Of course you also will be asked to write original papers. You will be given guidance in going through the steps used by successful writers. In fact, units 8 and 9 are totally devoted to helping you write your own generalization–specifics papers—the type required on many writing exams. But the sentence-arranging exercises will provide a foundation of experience with language and idea patterns that you can draw upon for these original papers.

Units 2, 4, 6, 7, 10, and 11 begin with a short introduction and then ask you to arrange sentences into papers. At the end of these units is a section called Analysis Of Papers. Read the analyses carefully because they highlight major features of the writing patterns focused on in the units. In fact, many important features are not mentioned in the unit introductions but only in the analyses, where they can be illustrated with examples from the papers you have already worked on. In unit 11, for instance, the difference between the denotative and connotative meanings of a word is only discussed in the analysis, after you have worked through a paper, "Stepparent Blues," illustrating the difference. Reading the analyses will teach you important concepts and techniques that you can use in your own writing.

Peer Response to Writing

For exercises in which you arrange jumbled sentences into a paper, your teacher might ask you to compare your arrangement with that of another student, and if there are any differences, discuss and explain why you believe your arrangement is better.

For exercises in which you write original papers, your teacher might suggest some or all of these activities.

1. Before starting to write, discuss the topic of the paper with one or several classmates to get ideas. You may take brief notes to remember key words and examples.
2. Write a first draft by yourself.
3. Exchange papers with another student and read each other's paper, or read your paper to a small group of classmates. Classmates will tell you what they like about your paper—its strong points— and also where you might express thoughts more clearly or add examples to support ideas.

   You respond in the same way to classmates' papers. First discuss the paper's strengths: its interesting introduction, insightful observations, good examples, well-constructed sentences, and appropriate conclusion. Then point to any sections which you find unclear, and make suggestions on how certain parts could be written more effectively or could use additional details.
4. Rewrite your paper based on any comments you found useful and any new ideas of your own.
5. Reread your entire paper to see whether it can be improved still further by adding more information or expressing points differently.
6. Proofread your paper for spelling and grammar errors. Reading a paper out loud often helps writers find such errors.

Unit

1

Combining And Rewriting Sentences

One of the most important abilities for good writing is the ability to write effective sentences. If your sentences are not well constructed, your writing will not impart the impressions you are trying to create. Read the following paragraph and consider the effect of its sentences.

A cat chased a lizard. The cat was big. The cat was fat. His fur was thick. The lizard was tiny. The lizard was a chameleon. A chameleon can change color. The color will be whatever the lizard touches. The lizard ran. It ran from place to place. It ran so fast. The colors even became confused. It was green. It should have been brown. It was red. It should have been grey. It was polka-dotted. It should have been striped. The lizard ran under the steps. It was safe. It would rest in the shade. The cat was frustrated. He yawned. He stretched. He curled up. He would sleep in the sun. This game would continue. It would continue the next time the cat saw the lizard.

What do you think about this paragraph? You must have noticed that the sentences lack style. They are all short and choppy, making the paragraph boring and immature sounding. The exercises in this unit will sharpen your skill to write powerful, informative sentences that hold the attention of your readers.

If you do not understand any of the grammatical terms used in this book, please refer to the Glossary.

Section 1   Adding Descriptive Words
(Adjectives & Adverbs) To A Sentence

Here is a pair of sentences that can be easily combined into one, more informative sentence.

The wolf bared its teeth.
The wolf was hungry.

Combined: The <u>hungry</u> wolf bared its teeth.

In this example, the second sentence provides a word (hungry) describing the wolf. The word "hungry" is simply added before the word "wolf" in the combined sentence. (A word like "wolf" that represents a thing is called a *noun*. A word like "hungry" that describes a thing is called an *adjective*.)

Two descriptive words can be added to a sentence by placing a comma between them, as shown in the next example.

A Cadillac stopped outside.
It was large and black.

Combined: A <u>large</u>, <u>black</u> Cadillac stopped outside.

comma   omit "and"

A word providing more detail about an action (verb) can also be added easily. (This type of word is an *adverb*.)

The man talked about his daughter.
He was talking proudly.

Combined: The man <u>proudly</u> talked about his daughter.

Note that a word adding more description about a thing is placed in front of the thing: The <u>blue</u> truck stopped. But a word adding more description about an action often can be placed either in front of or behind the main action word: The truck <u>quickly</u> stopped, or The truck stopped <u>quickly</u>. Use whichever position sounds and fits your meaning best.

The following exercises illustrate how information from as many as five simple sentences can be combined into one, richer sentence. Try the sample exercise before reading the answer below.

Sample Exercise

Combine the information from all four sentences into one sentence.

A mechanic sold her a car.
The mechanic was honest.
He sold it gladly.
The car was safe and economical.

Combined:

Here is how the sentences could be combined.

An <u>honest</u> mechanic <u>gladly</u> sold her a <u>safe</u>, <u>economical</u> car.
↑
comma

Now try the exercises.

EXERCISES

Instructions. Each exercise presents a main sentence and one or more sentences with additional descriptive details. Add the details to the main sentence, using the patterns illustrated above.

1. The hikers were glad to reach camp.
   They were tired.

   Combined:

2. A couch faced the door.
   It was new and red.

   Combined:

3. An intelligent, responsible adult learns that he cannot drink and drive. He learns it quickly.

   Combined:

4. The thief entered a house.
   He entered it quietly.
   The house was large and dark.

   Combined:

5. The woman bragged about her daughter.
   The woman was elderly.
   The bragging was done shamelessly.
   The daughter was financially successful.

   Combined:

6. A writer with knowledge can find a job writing brochures.
   The writer is skillful.
   The knowledge is technical.
   He or she can always find a job.
   The job is high paying.
   The brochures are commercial.

   Combined:

7. The horse jumped over the fence.
   The horse was grey.
   The jump was done gracefully.
   The fence was low and made of brick.

   Combined:

8. A child obeys relatives.
   The child is well-behaved.
   He or she promptly obeys.
   The relatives are adults.

   Combined:

9. Write three separate sentences that could be combined into one
   sentence. Then write the combined sentence.

Section 2   Adding Information With "Which"

*Part 1. Adding Extra (Nonessential) Details With
        "Which" and Commas*

In the last section you added simple one- or two-word descriptions to
sentences, as in this example.

The explosion injured 25 people.
It was a gas explosion.

Combined: The gas explosion injured 25 people.

If you wanted to give more information about the explosion, you could do it with the word "which" and commas like this.

The explosion injured 25 people.
The explosion was caused by a defective gas valve.

Combined: The explosion, which was caused by a defective gas valve, injured 25 people.

comma   comma

This method of adding information has the following general pattern.

The explosion, which ___EXTRA INFORMATION___ , injured 25 people. Note that the word "which" replaces "the explosion" in the second sentence when it is added to the first. Try the sample exercise before reading the answer below.

Sample Exercise

Add the information from the second sentence into the first sentence by using "which" and commas.

Her balancing skill drew cheers from the audience.
The skill came from years of practice.

Combined:

Here is how the sentences could be combined.

Combined: Her balancing skill, which came from years of practice, drew cheers from the audience.

Note that the word "which" replaces "the skill" in the second sentence when it is added to the first.

The skill came from years . . .

Her balancing skill, which came from years . . .

Note also that the first comma and "which" immediately follow the word "skill" in the combined sentence. ALWAYS put the first comma and "which" right after the word that you are giving more information about.

Now try the exercises

EXERCISES

Instructions. Each exercise presents two sentences. Add the information from the second sentence into the first sentence by using "which" and commas.

1. The Acme printing company went out of business.
   The company owed money to many people.

   Combined:

2. Pollen allows plants to reproduce.
   The pollen is carried from flower to flower by bees.

   Combined:

3. The Hawaiian Islands remain popular with tourists because of their mild climate and pleasant people.
   The Hawaiian Islands are located in the beautiful Pacific.

   Combined:

4. The novel <u>Oliver</u> <u>Twist</u> is about an orphan boy.
   It was written by Charles Dickens.

   Combined:

5. The mushrooms are poisonous.
   Bob found them in the woods.
   Hint: Drop the word "them" from the second sentence and put "which" before Bob.

   Combined:

Part 2. *Adding Essential Details With "Which" but NO Commas*

Compare the meaning of these two sentences. The only difference between them is that the first one has commas.

The bedroom, which has a green rug, is in the back of the house.
The bedroom which has a green rug is in the back of the house.

Which of these two sentences refers to a house with only one bedroom? The first sentence does. The commas indicate a pause or break in the sentence during which extra information is presented about "the bedroom." The second sentence suggests a house with several bedrooms, one of which has a green rug. There are no commas around "which has a green rug" because this is not extra information. It is essential in identifying which bedroom is in the back of the house.

The difference between the two situations can be seen from the simple sentences underlying the combined sentences.

The bedroom is in the back of the house.
The bedroom has a green rug.

Combined: The bedroom, which has a green rug, is in the back of the house.

One of the bedrooms is in the back of the house.
This bedroom has a green rug.

Combined: The bedroom which has the green rug is in the back of the house.

For the exercises that follow, the information added with "which" is essential in identifying an object, so commas should not be used. Try the sample exercise before reading the answer below.

Sample Exercise

Drop the word "certain" from the first sentence. Also drop "These companies" from the second sentence. Then add the information from the second sentence by using "which" but no commas.

Certain companies should be severely punished.
These companies violate anti-pollution laws.

Combined:

Here is how the sentences can be combined.

Combined: Companies which violate anti-pollution laws should be severely punished.

Notice that in the combined sentence the word "certain" is deleted because those particular companies are identified as the ones "which violate anti-pollution laws."

EXERCISES

Instructions. Add the information from the second sentence to the first by using "which" but no commas. Drop the word "certain."

1. Certain cars should be kept off the street.
These cars fail safety inspections.

Combined:

2. Certain typewriters are now available for less than $400.
   These typewriters can remember several lines of print.

   Combined:

3. Certain flowers cannot survive in low temperature.
   The flowers normally bloom in the summer.

   Combined:

4. Vocabulary. Pesticide: chemical used to kill pests such as insects.
   Certain pesticides are no longer used in farming.
   These pesticides have been proven harmful to humans.

   Combined:

5. Certain diseases are called zoonoses.
   These diseases are given to humans by animals.

   Combined:

6. A certain cat belongs to my cousin.
   It scratched me.

   Combined:

Here is how the sentences could be combined.

   The cat which scratched me belongs to my cousin.

Notice that the combined sentence begins "The cat" rather than "A cat" because it is talking about a specific cat, the one that scratched. Use this idea in the next two exercises.

7. A certain car has a dent in its right fender.
   The car hit the child.

   Combined:

8. A certain small plane is lost at sea.
   It took off at 3 o'clock.

   Combined:

FINAL NOTE. Sometimes you can use the word "that" instead of "which." "That" can be used when adding essential information (without commas) but not when adding extra information (with commas).

   The stories <u>which</u> Jim told were very funny.
   The stories <u>that</u> Jim told were very funny.

You can use "that" in your own writing whenever you are adding necessary information and "that" sounds better than "which."

Part 3. Omitting "Which" in Adding Details

Sometimes the word "which" can be omitted in adding extra (non-essential) details. Here is an example of two sentences combined with and without "which."

Manhattan Island is covered with skyscrapers from end to end.
It is the business capital of the world.

Combined: Manhattan Island, which is the business capital of
$\begin{bmatrix} \text{With} \\ \text{"Which"} \end{bmatrix}$ the world, is covered with skyscrapers from end to end.

Combined: Manhattan Island, the business capital of the world,
$\begin{bmatrix} \text{Without} \\ \text{"Which"} \end{bmatrix}$ is covered with skyscrapers from end to end.

Notice that "which is" has been deleted in the second combination, but the commas are retained because the added information is extra not essential. Now try the following exercises.

EXERCISES

Instructions. For each exercise, add the information from the second sentence to the first in two ways: 1. With commas and "which;" and 2. With commas but without "which was" or "which were."

1. Steel manufacturing has now become an important part of the Japanese economy.
   Steel manufacturing was once dominated by American capitalists.

   Combined:
   With
   "Which"

   Combined:
   Without
   "Which"

2. Beethoven's Ninth Symphony is a musical masterpiece that has been enjoyed by generations.
   It was written after the composer had gone deaf.

   Combined:

   Combined:

3. Teddy bears are irresistably lovable to young children and even some adults.
   Teddy bears were named after President Theodore "Teddy" Roosevelt.

   Combined:

   Combined:

Section 3   Adding Information With "Who"

Part 1. Adding Extra Details With "Who" and Commas

The word "who" can be used to add information to a sentence just like the word "which" was used in the last section. The only difference is that "who" is used for adding information about a person, whereas "which" is used for nonhuman things. Here is an example of how extra details can be added with "who" and commas.

Sarah Johnson won the race.
She is 24 years old.

Combined: Sarah Johnson, who is 24 years old, won the race.

Use the same pattern for combining the sentences in the following exercises.

EXERCISES

Instructions. Add the information from the second sentence to the first by using "who" and commas.

1. Mr. Hawkins wears a suit to work.
   He is a teacher.

   Combined:

2. Dr. Blake said Phil will be ready to play in the game Saturday.
   Dr. Blake is the team physician.

   Combined:

3. Benjamin Franklin was one of America's first scientists.
   He proved that lightning is electricity.

   Combined:

Part 2. Adding Essential Information With "Who" but NO Commas

When the information added with "who" is essential for identifying the person being discussed, then commas should not be used. Here is an example.

A certain lady was a scrub woman.
She won 3 million dollars in the lottery.

Combined: The lady who won 3 million dollars in the lottery was a scrubwoman.

Use the same pattern for combining the sentences in the following exercises.

EXERCISES

Instructions. Add the information from the second sentence to the first with "who" but no commas. Drop "certain" and add "the" to the beginning of the sentence when appropriate.

1. A certain football player weighs 215 pounds.
   He is doing push-ups.

   Combined:

2. A certain young lady pointed out the company's office.
   She runs the elevator.

   Combined.

3. Certain students tend to get good grades in tough courses.
   These students have learned to read carefully.

   Combined:

4. A certain player was born in Mexico City.
   He just hit a home run.

   Combined:

5. Certain people waste gas.
   These people use their cars to go just a few blocks.

   Combined:

6. Write any sentence using "who" to add information about a person.

   Combined:

Section 4   Combining Sentences Having The Same Subject Or Predicate

A complete sentence always has two parts: (a) A subject; and (b) Information about the subject (called the <u>predicate</u>). Here is an example.

<u>Willy</u> went to the store.

Subject   Predicate (information about the subject)

When two sentences have the same subject, they often can be combined into one sentence with the word "and" like this.

The ship hit a rock.
The ship started to sink.

Combined: The ship hit a rock and started to sink.

Three sentences with the same subject can be combined with commas and the word "and" like this.

The cookies in the jar are freshly baked.
The cookies in the jar are filled with chocolate chips.
The cookies in the jar are so soft they melt in your mouth.

Combined: The cookies in the jar are freshly baked, filled with chocolate chips, and so soft they melt in your mouth.

If two sentences have different subjects but the same predicate, they also may be combined with "and," as shown here.

Roses are used in making perfumes.
Violets are used in making perfumes.

Combined: Roses and violets are used in making perfumes.

Three sentences with different subjects but the same predicate can be combined by using commas along with "and."

Democrats want lower taxes.
Republicans want lower taxes.
Independents want lower taxes.

Combined: Democrats, Republicans, and Independents want lower taxes.

The following exercises illustrate additional opportunities for combining sentences with the same subject or predicate.

EXERCISES

Instructions. Combine the sentences in each exercise by using "and" along with any necessary commas. Use the examples just given as models.

1. Monsters live in the cellar.
   Monsters eat children.

   Combined:

2. Pauline wrapped the package in strong paper.
   Pauline took it to the post office.

   Combined:

3. John poured milk in a glass.
   John added a spoon of chocolate syrup.
   John stirred until the syrup was completely dissolved.

   Combined:

4. The mayor voted for the new traffic law.
   The city council voted for the new traffic law.

   Combined:

5. A police car raced down the street.
   A fire truck raced down the street.

   Combined:

6. A hot bath will make you feel better.
   A warm meal will make you feel better.
   A good rest will make you feel better.

   Combined:

7. The policeman drew his pistol.
   He kicked open the door.
   He charged into the room.

   Combined:

8. The quarterback studied the plays.
   He practiced them for hours.
   He executed them perfectly at the game.

   Combined:

9. Use "then" instead of "and" to combine these sentences.
   Gwen opened the can.
   Gwen emptied the contents into a red bowl.
   Gwen put the bowl on the floor for the cat.

   Combined:

10. Write any sentence with one subject and two predicates connected by "and."

11. Write any sentence with two subjects connected by "and" and one predicate.

Section 5   Combining Sentences With AND, OR, BUT, or SO And A Comma

The last section dealt with combining sentences sharing a subject or predicate. But two sentences may be related even when they have different subjects and predicates. Often such sentences can be combined by showing the relation between them with AND, OR, BUT, or SO. A comma is included when these coordinating conjunctions are used to join sentences. Here is a definition and example for each.

AND: Used for just adding one piece of information to another, <u>without</u> showing any special relationship.

   Jack made a salad.
   Gloria baked a cake.

Combined: Jack made a salad, and Gloria baked a cake.

   Comma necessary because two separate sentences are being joined by "and."

OR: Used for joining sentences presenting two possibilities.

   You must make your car payments. ←
   The bank will take your car. ←   2 possibilities
Combined: You must make your car payments, or the bank will take
          your car.

BUT: Used to show a <u>contrast</u> between two ideas.

Harold bought some oranges.
His wife had told him to buy tangerines.

Combined: Harold bought some oranges, but his wife had told him to buy tangerines.

SO: Used to show a reason–result relation.

The car would not start. (Reason)
I took the bus. (Result)

Combined: The car would not start, so I took the bus.

Refer to these definitions and examples in doing the following exercises.

EXERCISES

Instructions. Combine the two sentences in each exercise with a comma and one of the four words: AND, OR, BUT, SO.

Several exercises say: Do not use AND. Use one of the other three words. They are more powerful for showing relationships between ideas.

1. It was a hot summer day.
   Linda went for a swim in the pool.
   Do not use AND.

   Combined:

2. Bill and Judy got married.
   Their parents wanted them to wait another year.
   Do not use AND.

   Combined:

3. The leaves are falling from the trees.
   The birds are flying south.

   Combined:

4. Stronger laws must be passed to stop air pollution.
   There will be no clean air left to breathe.

   Combined:

5. I don't like any rock bands.
   My brother is crazy about the Rolling Stones.

   Combined:

6. The company will give your job back.
   Otherwise, the union will call a strike.
   Hint: Drop "otherwise"

   Combined:

7. All the seats in the bus were taken.
   Judy had to stand.

   Combined:

8. You can have a new bicycle.
   Otherwise, your sister can have a new portable stereo.

   Combined:

9. John is less than 6 feet tall.
   He is the highest scorer on the basketball team.
   Don't use AND.

   Combined:

10. The weather forecast was for frost.
    People covered their plants or brought them inside.
    Don't use AND.

    Combined:

11. Write a sentence composed of two sentences connected with a comma and "but."

12. Write a sentence composed of two sentences connected with a comma and "so."

13. Write a sentence composed of two sentences connected with a comma and "or."

FINAL NOTE. The words "and," "but," "so," and "or" are called con-junctions. One use of these words is to prevent a type of error known as a run-on-sentence. Here is an example.

Incorrect: The boys scored higher on the math test the girls
⌈Run-On ⌉scored higher on the reading test.
⌊Sentence⌋

This is really two complete sentences, but one runs into the other be-cause they are not separated by appropriate punctuation. To correct such an error, use a comma and a conjunction or write two separate sentences.

Correct: The boys scored higher on the math test, <u>but</u> the girls scored higher on the reading text.

Correct: The boys scored higher on the math test. The girls scored higher on the reading test.

Section 6   Combining Sentences With HOWEVER, THEREFORE, Or MOREOVER And A Semicolon

HOWEVER, THEREFORE, and MOREOVER are adverbial conjunctions that can be used in the same way that BUT, SO, and AND were used in the last section. But with these adverbial conjunctions you must use a semicolon before the conjunction and a comma after it.

<u> Sentence 1 </u> ; adverbial conjunction, <u> Sentence 2   </u>

Examples

I like Joe; however, I love Jim.

I went to see that movie yesterday; therefore, I'd rather go skating today.

Jeff brought all of his grades up this semester; moreover, he became captain of the school football team.

If you read these sentences carefully, you will see that HOWEVER is used like BUT; THEREFORE is equal to SO; and MOREOVER means the same as AND. These conjunctive adverbs add variety and maturity to your writing; therefore, use them whenever they seem appropriate in your own papers.

EXERCISES

Instructions. Combine the following sentences using HOWEVER (but), THEREFORE (so), or MOREOVER (and). Do not forget the semicolon and comma.

1. This winter has been cold.
   Last winter was colder.

   Combined:

2. Elaine prepared thoroughly for the test by studying many hours.
   She was able to answer every question correctly.

   Combined:

3. The Bank of America donated $25,000 to help the flood victims.
   The Red Cross provided food and shelter.

   Combined:

4. Mary wants to visit Boston.
   She cannot find anyone to take care of her cats.

   Combined:

5. Ducks cannot survive in extremely cold weather.
   They must fly south in the winter to find warmer temperatures.

   Combined:

Section 7   Combining Sentences With Prepositional Phrases

Prepositions are words like "in," "under," "after," "to," "of," and "without" that are used to describe relationships between things, such as spatial and time relationships. Here is a sentence with three prepositions underlined.

Bob went to the store in the truck after dinner.

A prepositional phrase is a phrase starting with a preposition. In the above sentence, the three prepositional phrases are:

to the store
in the truck
after dinner

Combining prepositional phrases is one way to lengthen sentences. The prepositional phrases are underlined in the following examples.

Example 1.

The new girl sat by Bob.
They sat on the sofa.
The sofa was near the window.

Combined: The new girl sat by Bob on the sofa near the window.

Example 2.

The young boy was racing.
He was racing <u>across the glistening ice.</u>
He was <u>from the hockey club.</u>
He was racing <u>with new skates.</u>

Combined: The young boy from the hockey club was racing across the glistening ice with new skates.

Note that "from the hockey club" is placed after "boy" and "across the glistening ice" is placed after "racing." Place prepositional phrases where the information they add will be understood most clearly.

Now try these exercises.

EXERCISES

Instructions. For each exercise, lengthen the first sentence by adding the prepositional phrases from the other sentences. Here are the prepositions to look for.

in, with, from, under, after, for, to, on, during, of, next, across

1. The boat sank.
   The boat was in the harbor.
   It sank with the diamonds still aboard.

   Combined:

2. Juanita got the pistol and bullets.
   She got them from the shoe box.
   The shoe box is under the bed.
   She did this after Willy left.
   He left for work.

   Combined:

3. The teacher sent Bob upstairs when she caught him writing.
   She sent him to the principal's office.
   She sent him with a note.
   The note was in a sealed envelope.
   He was writing on the wall.
   He was writing in black crayon.
   It was during recess.

   Combined:

4. John is on the roof.
   It is the roof of a truck.
   He is with dad.
   The truck is in the driveway.
   The driveway is next door.

   Combined:

5. Glenn rides the bicycle every weekday morning.
   It is the one with the thin wheels and broken lamp.
   He rides it to his store.
   His store is in the city.
   Suggestion: Let your combined sentence end with
   "weekday morning."

   Combined:

6. A flock flew lazily.
   It was a flock of pelicans.
   They flew in a straight line.
   They flew across the horizon.
   They were on their way home.

   Combined:

Section 8   Adding A Prepositional Phrase To The Beginning Of A Sentence

Remember from the last section that prepositions are words such as "in," "with" and "without." Sometimes a prepositional phrase may be placed at the beginning of a sentence. Generally a comma is placed after such a prepositional phrase. Here are two examples.

Example 1.

Thieves cut the fence and stole four race horses.
They did it <u>in the middle of the night</u>.

Combined: In the middle of the night, thieves cut the fence and stole four race horses.

Example 2.

We got drenched running from the bus stop to the office.
We ran <u>without the protection of an umbrella.</u>

Combined: Without the protection of an umbrella, we got drenched
running from the bus stop to the office.

Now try these exercises.

EXERCISES

Instructions. Each exercise has two sentences. Add the information from the second sentence to the beginning of the first sentence, starting with one of these prepositions: under, in, without, with, inside.

1. Wolves entered the pasture and killed three sheep.
They did it under the cover of darkness.

Combined:

2. You should explain why your topic is important.
This should be done in the introduction of a paper.

Combined:

3. The miners were asphyxiated when an explosion released poisonous gas into the shaft where they were working.
The miners worked without the protection of gas masks.

Combined:

4. The detectives kicked open the door and charged into the apartment.
They did this with their guns drawn.

Combined:

5. Three firefighters were trying to free a man pinned under a collapsed wall.
They were inside the burning building.

Combined:

6. The young man received the maximum sentence possible for his crime.
He stood trial without the benefit of a good lawyer.

Combined:

Section 9 Using BEFORE, AFTER, or WHEN To Show Time Relationships

The words BEFORE, AFTER, and WHEN can be used to combine sentences by showing the time relationship between events. Here is an example.

Julie burned dinner twice.
Maria decided to do all the cooking.

Combined 1: <u>Before</u> Maria decided to do all the cooking, Julie burned dinner twice.

Combined 2: Julie burned dinner twice <u>before</u> Maria decided to do all the cooking.

Notice that you have a choice between two sentence patterns in joining sentences with <u>before</u>.

1. <u>Before</u> in front and a comma in the middle.
2. <u>Before</u> in the middle and NO comma.

The word "after" means the opposite of "before." The above sentences could be combined with "after" this way.

Julie burned dinner twice.
Maria decided to do all the cooking.

Combined 1: <u>After</u> Julie burned dinner twice, Maria decided to do all the cooking.

Combined 2: Maria decided to do all the cooking <u>after</u> Julie burned dinner twice.

The word "when" can be used to show that one event occurred just before and caused another event.

He lost his job.
He applied for unemployment benefits.

Combined 1: <u>When</u> he lost his job, he applied for unemployment benefits.

Combined 2: He applied for unemployment benefits <u>when</u> he lost his job.

The following exercises present additional illustrations of how "before," "after," and "when" can be used to combine sentences.

EXERCISES

Instructions. Each exercise presents two sentences and a word to combine them. Use both sentence patterns just shown, namely:

1. "Before" (after, when) in front and a comma in the middle.
2. "Before" (after, when) in the middle and NO comma.

1. Use AFTER

   The pool was drained.

   The workman repaired and painted the bottom.

   Combined 1:

   Combined 2:

2. Use BEFORE

   The gasoline engine had to be invented.

   The modern automobile could be produced.

   Combined 1:

   Combined 2:

3. Use WHEN

   The lake freezes.

   The temperature drops.

   Combined 1:

   Combined 2:

4. Use WHEN

   The lunch whistle blew.

   The machines stopped and the employees hurried to the cafeteria.

   Combined 1:

   Combined 2:

5. Vocabulary

   Arson: starting fires to destroy property illegally

   Use the word (before, or after, or when) and sentence pattern that you judge to be best.

   The firemen put out the fire.

   The inspector checked the burned building for evidence of arson.

   Combined:

6. Use the word (before, or after, or when) and sentence pattern that you judge to be best.

   A plane is permitted to take off from a large airport.

   The control tower scans the area to be sure the flight path is clear.

   Combined:

7. Write a sentence beginning with "before."

8. Write a sentence beginning with "after."

9. Write a sentence with "after" in the middle.

10. Write a sentence which begins with "when" and which does not ask a question.

11. Write a sentence with "when" in the middle.

Section 10   Combining Sentences With BECAUSE Or SINCE

The word BECAUSE can be used to join a pair of sentences stating a cause–effect relation. Here is an example.

Brian fell asleep smoking.
The bed caught fire.

Combined 1: <u>Because</u> Brian fell asleep smoking, the bed caught fire.

Combined 2: The bed caught fire <u>because</u> Brian fell asleep smoking.

Notice that you have a choice between two sentence patterns in joining sentences with because.

1. <u>Because</u> in front and a comma in the middle.
2. <u>Because</u> in the middle and NO comma.

Notice also that "because" is always placed right before the sentence giving the <u>cause</u>. If "because" is placed at the beginning of the combined sentence, then the <u>cause</u> comes first, and the effect follows the comma.

Because Brian fell asleep smoking, the bed caught fire.

           Cause   Effect

But if "because" is placed in the middle, then the cause follows at the end.

The bed caught fire because Brian fell asleep smoking.

           Effect   Cause

One meaning of the word "since" is "because." "Since" can be used like "because" in combining sentences:

The door was locked.
The firemen entered through the window.

Combined 1: <u>Since</u> the door was locked, the firemen entered through the window.

Combined 2: The firemen entered through the window <u>since</u> the door was locked.

For the following exercises, you will only use "because" in combining sentences. However, use "since" in your own writing whenever it sounds best.

EXERCISES

Instructions. For each exercise, combine the sentences using "because" and both patterns shown in the exercises just given, namely:

1. "Because" in front and a comma between the sentences.
2. "Because" in the middle and NO comma.

1. The weather improved.
   The plane was able to take off.

   Combined 1:

   Combined 2:

2. We turned off the electric heater.
   The office got too warm.

   Combined 1:

   Combined 2:

3. We turned on the electric heater.
   The office got too warm.

   Combined 1:

   Combined 2:

4. The car skidded uncontrollably and struck a tree.
   The street was a sheet of ice.

   Combined 1:

   Combined 2:

5. Little children may run unexpectedly into the street.
   The policewoman is especially watchful of little children.
   Note: You may substitute "they" or "them" for "little chil-
       dren" where appropriate.

   Combined 1:

   Combined 2:

6. Write a sentence beginning with "because."

7. Write a sentence with "because" in the middle.

Section 11   Adding A Participle Phrase
(With A Comma) To The Beginning Of A Sentence

In section 2 you combined sentences like this.

The pool water felt pleasantly warm.
The pool water was <u>heated by the sun.</u>

Combined: The pool water, heated by the sun, felt pleasantly warm.

The information from the second sentence also could be added to
the first sentence this way.

Combined: <u>Heated by the sun,</u> the pool water felt pleasantly warm.

A group of words like "heated by the sun" is called a participle phrase. Try adding the underlined participle phrase in the sample exercise before reading the answer below.

Sample Exercise

Add the information from the second sentence to the first as a phrase at the beginning (with a comma).

Linda trembled in the closet.
Linda was terrified by the lightning outside.

Combined:

Here is how the sentences could be combined.

Combined: Terrified by the lightning outside, Linda trembled in the closet.

Now try the following exercises.

EXERCISES

Instructions. Add the information from the second sentence to the first as a phrase at the beginning (with a comma).

1. Fred left the restaurant and drove to another one.
   Fred was disgusted by the dirty silverware.

   Combined:

2. The burglar ran back to his car.
   The burglar was frightened by a watchdog.

   Combined:

3. Men from all over the country rushed to California in 1849.
   They were drawn by the discovery of gold.

   Combined:

4. Paula burst out in tears.
   She was disappointed about losing the contest.

   Combined:

5. The policewoman wrote out a $50 ticket.
   She was smiling at the flimsy excuse the driver had given for speeding.

   Combined:

6. Write a sentence beginning with a descriptive phrase.

Avoid Dangling Modifiers

When attaching a descriptive phrase to the beginning of a sentence, beware of producing a dangling modifier. What is wrong with this sentence?

Painted red with yellow flames, Fred proudly drove his new hot rod up and down the strip.

The sentence suggests that Fred was painted red with yellow flames.

Here are two better ways to express the same idea.

Fred proudly drove his new hot rod, painted red with yellow flames, up and down the strip.

Painted red with yellow flames, Fred's new hot rod was an eye-catching sight as Fred proudly drove up and down the strip.

In general, try to place a descriptive phrase as close as possible to the thing being described. If you place a descriptive phrase at the beginning of a sentence, be sure the thing described immediately follows it.

To check your understanding of dangling modifiers, read the following two sentences and write dangling modifier in front of the one containing a dangling modifier.

_____ Tired and hungry, the camp was a welcome sight for the hiker.

_____ Tired and hungry, the hikers were glad when the camp was in sight.

Section 12   Active And Passive Forms Of Sentences

This section shows you how to add variety to your sentences and make certain types of weak, wordy sentences stronger.

A common type of sentence has the following pattern.

An <u>actor</u> acted on an <u>object</u>.

Here is an example.

<u>John</u> kicked the <u>ball</u>.
actor ↑ object
acted on

A sentence with this pattern is called an ACTIVE sentence. By contrast, the same idea can be expressed in a sentence with a different pattern called PASSIVE. Here is the passive pattern.

An <u>object</u> was acted on by an <u>actor</u>.

The <u>ball</u> was kicked by <u>John</u>.
object   actor
was acted on by

The "actor" in these sentences need not be a person. It can be a mechanical device, an emotion, or anything that has an effect on something else (the object). Furthermore, the "object" does not have to be a physical thing. Here are two examples.

Example 1.

ACTIVE: The <u>truck</u> carried <u>watermelons</u>.
actor ↑ object
acted on

PASSIVE: <u>Watermelons</u> were carried by the <u>truck</u>.
object   actor
were acted on by

Example 2.

ACTIVE: <u>Jealousy</u> destroys <u>good friendships</u>.
      actor   ↑   object
          acts on

PASSIVE: <u>Good friendships</u> are destroyed by <u>jealousy</u>.
      object   actor
          are acted on by

Notice that active sentences put the actor at the beginning. The word passive means inactive. Passive sentences put the inactive thing (the object) at the beginning. Notice also that passive sentences are longer because they contain phrases like "was kicked by" rather than just "kicked," and "are destroyed by" rather than just "destroys." The extra words can make passive sentences slower and duller reading.

Weak writers often use too many passive sentences. Strong writers have learned that active sentences are crisper and carry more punch. Try to use mostly active sentences in your writing. Use passive sentences only when you want to draw attention to the object acted on, or when you want to add variety to your sentence patterns.

Try the following sample exercise before reading the answer.

Sample Exercise

Instructions. Rewrite the following passive sentence as an active sentence with the same meaning.

Passive: Interesting entertainment is provided by television.

Active: _____

For this sentence, <u>television</u> is the actor, <u>provides</u> is the action, and <u>interesting entertainment</u> is the object of the action. Therefore the active sentence has this form.

Active: Television provides interesting entertainment.

Now begin the exercises.

EXERCISES

Set 1

Instructions. Rewrite each of the passive sentences as an active sentence with the same meaning.

1. Passive: That house was owned by Michael Jackson.

   Active: _____

2. Passive: The plane was flown by a young pilot.

   Active: _____

3. Passive: Bodyweight is increased by overeating.

   Active: _____

4. Passive: The food and entertainment were paid for by a local radio station.

   Active: _____

Set 2

Instructions. The following sentences are a little more complicated, so the first exercise has been answered as an illustration. Try the first exercise before reading the answer.

1. Passive: The ball was hit by Bob into the stands.

   Active: _____

Here is the answer.

Active: Bob hit the ball into the stands.

2. Passive: Five silver coins were taken by Denise when the guard turned his back.

   Active:_____

3. Passive: A dozen roses were bought by Lester for Pauline.

   Active: _____

Here are two correct answers for exercise 3.

   Active: Lester bought a dozen roses for Pauline.
   Active: Lester bought Pauline a dozen roses.

Both sentences begin with the actor (Lester), so they are both active. Write two active sentences for the remaining exercises in this set. Use the answers for exercise 3 as a model.

4. Passive: The Chevy was left by Santa for Barbara.

   Active: _____

   Active: _____

5. Passive: A poem was read by Fred to Cynthia.

   Active: _____

   Active: _____

Caution: Read the next two exercises carefully to pinpoint the ACTOR.

6. Passive: Free tickets are provided to guests by the hotel.

   Active: _____

7. Passive: The note was sent to all teachers by the art department.

   Active: _____

Set 3

Sometimes you may use passive sentences to emphasize the object rather than the actor. For example, in writing a paper for a home economics course, you might use this active sentence: A poor diet weakens the body's resistance to disease. But if you were writing for people concerned about illness, the passive form of the sentence could be more effective in catching their interest: The body's resistance to disease is weakened by a poor diet.

Instructions. Rewrite each of the following active sentences in passive form.

1. Active: Clinton ate an apple.

   Passive: _____

2. Active: Smoking reduces your lung capacity.

   Passive: _____

3. Active: Several people witnessed the horrible crime.

   Passive: _____

4. Try to write two passive forms for this sentence.

   Active: Mrs. Cooke donated 20 cakes to the charity party.

   Passive: _____

   Passive: _____

5. a. Write any sentence in active form.
   b. Write the same sentence in passive form.

Unit Summary

This unit presented some of the major patterns used in writing rich, interesting sentences. There are other patterns that also can be used for combining information into sentences. You will see examples of them in your general reading and in the remaining units of this text. Now that you have completed Unit 1, you have developed a sensitivity to the way writers create sentences. As you discover new sentence patterns, use them to express yourself effectively in writing.

For a final exercise, rewrite the choppy paragraph presented at the beginning of this unit.

Unit

2

Physical Description: Creating Word Pictures

Creating "word pictures" is a basic form of writing. How does something look? Where is it located? What does it sound, feel, or taste like? Through a careful choice of words you can recreate for readers the sights and other sensory impressions you have experienced.

Being able to write vivid descriptions is an important skill for writing the various types of papers covered in later units. For example, in unit 6 on classification, different types of cheeses are described in terms of how they look, taste, and smell. Similarly, when you are comparing two things (unit 10) or arguing a position (units 8 and 9), you must be able to describe people, objects, and situations to make your ideas clear and concrete.

The key to writing a strong description is taking the time to include plenty of details so your reader gets a full picture of the person or situation you are describing. Instead of just writing, "The man was smoking," you can fuel your reader's imagination with additional details like, "The man was puffing nervously on a long, thin cigarette." Don't just write, "The car drove very fast down the street." Tell the reader how fast: "The car sped down the street at over 80 mph." Here are some other examples.

Vague	*Detailed*
a high salary	$75,000 a year
a youngster	a 3-year-old
a big car	a Lincoln
very hot day	over 100 degrees
is a big man	is 6'5" and weighs 280 lbs

Such details help a reader visualize the impressions you are trying to communicate. The exercises that follow sharpen your skill in writing descriptions of people and situations.

Writing For Learning

Many of the following exercises ask you to write sentences in the best logical order. To obtain the greatest benefit, do not copy the words letter-by-letter. Instead, use these steps for each sentence.

1. Read as many words as you believe you can write correctly from memory (usually five to 10 words).

2. Write those words from memory, including all capitals and punctuation marks.

3. Check back to the original sentence and correct any errors you made.

4. Read the next group of words and repeat the above steps.

Generally you will be able to read, memorize, and correctly write between five and 10 words. Sometimes you may be able to remember an entire simple sentence correctly. But with a large, difficult-to-spell word, you may only try to write that one word correctly from memory. Writing from memory will make you more aware of the spelling, grammar, punctuation, and word patterns used in standard written English.

SET 1. WRITING DIRECTIONS FOR A DRIVER

If friends are coming to a party at your home or they are meeting you downtown to see a show, you might have to write driving directions. This is one of the simplest forms of description, but your directions must be clear so the driver won't get lost.

Exercise 1. The following sentences refer to the map. Number the sentences so they are arranged into directions for getting from the corner of Adams and Oak to the movie theatre.

_____ Go two blocks, which will bring you to the end of the road, and make a left onto Blossom.

_____ You will come to a fork in the road, where you should take the left branch, putting you on Spruce.

_____ Drive west along Oak St. to the first light and make a left.

_____ Drive for two blocks and you will see the movie theatre.

_____ When you get to the Texaco station, bear right onto L Avenue.

_____ Go straight until you pass over the railroad tracks, then at the next corner make a right.

Exercise 2. Write the sentences in the order you number them to form directions for getting from the corner of Adams and Oak to the movie theatre.

Exercise 3. A friend wants to drive from the bowling alley to Turner Ct. at night when it will be hard to read street signs. Write directions using these easy-to-see landmarks: fire station, fork in the road, AAA Restaurant, Star Motel, and bridge over stream. Remember to mention in which direction your friend should start driving along Central Ave.

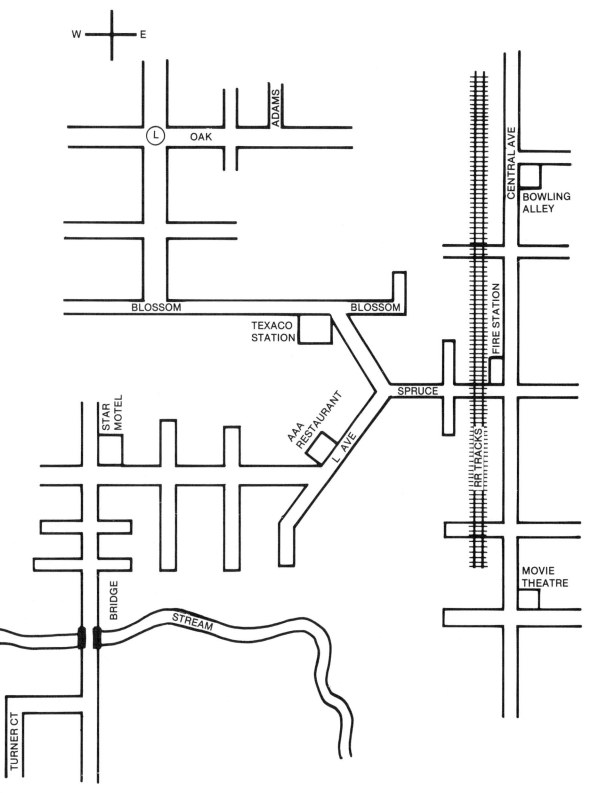

SET 2. DESCRIPTION OF BUFFET TABLE

The following sentences can be arranged into an orderly description of this buffet table.

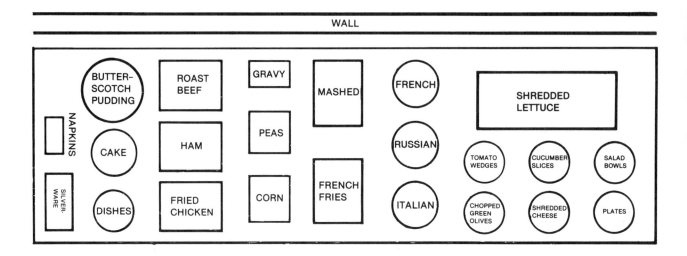

Exercise 1. Number the sentences so they systematically describe the buffet table, starting with the table's location and then moving from one end to the other.

_____ Next to these plates is the salad section.

_____ Moving past the salad dressings, you come to two pans of potatoes: mashed in back and French fried in front.

_____ The buffet table is against the wall, so you can only serve yourself from the front.

_____ There is a large tub of shredded lettuce toward the back of the table, and in front there are four bowls with salad accompaniments: tomato wedges, cucumber slices, chopped green olives, and shredded cheese.

_____ As you face the table, a stack of dinner plates and another stack of salad bowls are located at the right end.

_____ Finally, at the left end of the table there is a pile of napkins and a box with silverware.

_____ To the left of this are three metal containers with salad dressings: French closest to the wall, Russian in the middle, and Italian nearest the front.

_____ Next to the mashed potatoes is a pan of gravy, in front of this is a pan of peas, and closest to the front a pan of corn.

_____ This brings you to the desserts.

_____ To the left of these vegetables are three large meat trays, with roast beef in the back, fried chicken in front, and ham between them.

_____ There is a large bowl of butterscotch pudding toward the back of the table, a platter of chocolate cake slices in the middle, and a stack of dessert dishes in front.

Exercise 2. Write the sentences in the order you numbered them to form a systematic description of the buffet table.

Exercise 3. A picture of the buffet table has been reprinted on page 222. With all material from exercises 1 and 2 put away, write a systematic description of the table, starting with its location and then following the path of a person moving from one end to the other.

SET 3. HOLIDAY COOKIES

In the last two sets of exercises you described the locations of things. Now you will begin describing things themselves.

On holidays, bakeries sell special cookies in shapes and colors fitting the occasion. For Christmas, green cookies shaped like Christmas trees, with pink candy sprinkles for lights, might be displayed in the window. Writing descriptions of such cookies is the topic of these exercises.

Exercise 1. For each holiday, write a sentence describing the type of cookie a bakery might display. Let all your sentences have this form.

For <u>holiday,</u> <u>color</u> cookies shaped like <u>object,</u> with <u>color</u> candy sprinkles for <u>details on object,</u> are displayed in bakery windows.

Example 1.

For <u>Christmas,</u> <u>green</u> cookies shaped like <u>Christmas trees,</u> with <u>silver</u> candy sprinkles for <u>lights,</u> are displayed in bakery windows.

Example 2.

For <u>Christmas,</u> <u>red</u> cookies shaped like <u>Santa Claus,</u> with <u>white and black</u> candy sprinkles for <u>the beard, facial features, buttons, and belt,</u> are displayed in bakery windows.

Note that two candy colors, black and white, are used to paint details on Santa. Use as many colors as necessary to describe cookies for the following holidays.

Halloween: _____

_____

Valentine's Day: _____

Exercise 2. Here is a different description of a holiday cookie.

At Halloween, bakeries sell orange, pumpkin-shaped cookies having facial features drawn with yellow frosting.

Write a description of an Easter cookie in a form similar to this.

Exercise 3. With all materials from exercises 1 and 2 put away, write descriptions of cookies for any two holidays (e.g., Thanksgiving, Fourth of July).

SET 4. THUMBNAIL DESCRIPTION OF A MAN

Exercise 1. Number the sentences to describe a man in the following order: overall body (size, type), face, grooming (hair, clothes), general impression.

Vocabulary

vitality: health and energy

____ His hair was fashionably cut and his clothes had been carefully chosen in a fine men's shop.

____ The young, new manager was tall and muscular.

____ He was the picture of confidence and success.

____ He had high cheek bones, a strong jaw, and brown eyes that seemed to glow with vitality.

Exercise 2. Write the sentences in the order you numbered them to describe a man in terms of overall body type, face, grooming, and general impression.

Exercise 3. With all material from exercise 1 and 2 put away, write a brief description of a friend or relative in terms of body type, face, grooming, general impression, and any other characteristics you consider important.

SET 5. ILLUSTRATING PERSONALITY TRAITS

When you describe a person with broad words like "cheerful" or "ambitious," you can help your reader understand what you mean by also describing some actions of the person that show cheerfulness or ambitiousness. This exercise presents brief descriptions of actions illustrating personality traits.

Exercise 1. Following are five sentences stating that a person has a certain personality trait. On the next page are five descriptions of actions illustrating the personality traits. Decide which description fits each personality trait, then write the descriptions in the spaces by the traits below.

Kathleen is ambitious. _____

_____

_____

Paula is cheerful. _____

_____

_____

Gwen has a good sense of humor. _____

_____

_____

Linda is considerate. _____

_____

_____

Louise is devoted to her children. _____

_____

_____

She enjoys hearing new jokes. She often makes her friends laugh by imitating someone they know or by seeing the funny side of a situation.

She always says something friendly when you meet her. She doesn't complain about much and is seldom depressed.

She tries never to disturb people by turning on her stereo too loud or too early. When she puts on a TV program or buys something like ice cream, she takes other people's tastes into account.

She is always ready to drop what she is doing and play with her 4-year-old daughter or help her 11-year-old son with homework and other problems. She spends little on herself but puts all the family's extra money into a savings account for the children's education.

She studies for 3 hours every evening during the week and for 5 hours a day on weekends because she wants to earn a high grade point average and eventually become a lawyer.

Exercise 2. Think of a friend or relative with a personality trait like generosity, greediness, dishonesty, calmness, etc. Write a description of his or her actions and attitudes illustrating the trait.

SET 6. DESCRIPTION BY COMPARISON

A good way to help your reader visualize something you are describing is to compare it to something else that is already familiar. This is illustrated in the following exercise.

Exercise 1. Number the sentences within each paragraph to form the best logical order. Some sentences have already been numbered.

Vocabulary

counterpart: something similar to another thing but in a different situation
nutritious: having food value useful to the body
structure: form, the parts something is made of
substances: materials
visualize: picture mentally

Paragraph I

_____ A kernel of wheat is about the size of a grain of rice.

_____ Why is whole wheat bread more nutritious than white bread?

_____ But the structure of a wheat kernel can be visualized better by comparing it to something larger and easier to see, such as an egg.

_____ To answer this question, it is necessary to examine a kernel of wheat.

Paragraph II

_____ A kernel of wheat also has three parts.

_____ An egg has three parts: shell, white, and yolk.

_3_ Its covering (shell) is called the bran.

_____ Thus, the three parts of a wheat kernel are the bran, endosperm, and germ.

_____ The counterpart of an egg's yolk is called the kernel's germ.

_____ What corresponds to the white of an egg is called the endosperm of a wheat kernel.

Paragraph III

_____ Only the endosperm is then used to produce white flour for making appealing baked goods.

_2_ Therefore, the endosperm is separated from the bran and germ in a process called milling.

_____ Bakers have found that the endosperm makes the smoothest, tastiest bread and cake.

_4_ Unfortunately, the bran and germ contain more vitamins, fiber, and other healthy substances than the endosperm.

_____ For this reason, whole wheat bread is more nutritious.

_____ Whole wheat flour keeps all three parts of the wheat kernel.

Exercise 2. Write the sentences in the order you numbered them to form a paper that includes a description of a wheat kernel illustrated through comparison with an egg.

Exercise 3. Write the following list of facts on a separate sheet of paper. Then put away all other material from exercises 1 and 2, and write a short paper explaining why whole wheat bread is more nutritious than white bread. Include a description of a wheat kernel illustrated through comparison with an egg.

bran — shell
endosperm — white
germ — yolk
endosperm — used to make white flour for smoother, tastier bread and cake
milling — separating endosperm from bran and germ
bran & germ — more vitamins, fiber, and other healthy substances

SET 7. THE SCHOOL CAFETERIA

Do you like your school cafeteria? Some school cafeterias are quite good, but others are a disappointment. The following exercises contain a description of a school cafeteria that could use improvement.

Exercise 1. In planning a paper on the school cafeteria, the following ideas might come to mind.

> short hours, long line, overcooked vegetables, stale desserts, greasy hamburgers, small portions, everything lukewarm, unfriendly staff, crowded seating, noisy, disgusting pile-up of dirty dishes, too expensive.

To organize these ideas into a paper, you could group them into the following categories. Write each item from the above list in an appropriate category. The first item has already been written.

Poor service in obtaining food: _____short hours,_____

Poor food: _____

Unpleasant atmosphere while eating: _____

Bad value (pay much, get little): _____

Exercise 2. Ideas about the cafeteria from the previous exercise are contained in the following sentences. Number the sentences within each paragraph to form the best logical order.

Vocabulary
consensus: agreement
endure: suffer, tolerate, put up with
miniscule: tiny
resent: become offended (insulted) and angry

Paragraph I

__2__ For one thing, the hours are too short.

_____ There is a consensus among students that the school cafeteria stinks.

__4__ This means if you were too rushed to have breakfast, you can't get a bite of food to quiet your growling stomach until noon.

_____ The cafeteria doesn't open until 12:00 o'clock, and it closes immediately at 1:30.

_____ Or if you are busy with a school assignment during the brief period it is open, you totally miss lunch.

_____ A second problem is the long waiting line.

_____ If you only have a half hour for lunch, there is no point going to the cafeteria because you may not get through the long line in time to eat.

__7__ Due partly to the short hours and partly to an inefficient cashier who constantly chats with the lady that makes coffee and replaces desserts, the waiting line is always long and slow.

_____ A third complaint is the unfriendliness of the staff.

_____ Furthermore, the salad lady gets irritated and rude if you ask her to look in the refrigerator for a dish of cottage cheese or something else not available on the shelf.

_____ Instead, she dumps the food on your plate as if she resents serving students.

_____ The lady serving the hot food never smiles.

Paragraph II

_____ It is all the same lukewarm temperature.

_____ When you do get your food, you wonder whether the long wait and unpleasant service were worth enduring.

__2__ First, the hot food isn't very hot, and the cold food isn't very cold.

_____ The meatloaf is lukewarm, the vegetables are lukewarm, and the jellos and puddings are lukewarm.

__5__ What makes the food even more tasteless is that the cooked foods are overcooked and the desserts are usually stale.

__7__ And the slices of cake are so dry that it is rumored they are gotten from a supermarket after sitting unbought on the shelf for several days.

_____ The string beans and carrots don't have a trace of crispness or sweetness left, as if they were boiled for hours.

_9_ The buns are crusty with age, while the meat patties are thin as crackers and dripping with grease.

_____ Even the old American standby, the hamburger, is a total loss.

Paragraph III

_____ Also, the conveyor belt where you are supposed to place dirty dishes is often backed up, creating a disgusting pile of trays, soiled plates, and spilled food.

_____ The tables are cramped together, so you hear all the conversations and noise from neighboring eaters.

_____ The atmosphere in the cafeteria is another disappointment.

_6_ Furthermore, the servings are miniscule, especially the meat portions which are about the size of the children's portions sold at reduced prices in other cafeterias.

_____ Added to all of this are the outrageous prices.

_____ The unavoidable conclusion is that the cafeteria requires new management to make it an efficient, pleasant place to eat.

_____ A Pepsi costs 75¢ and a hamburger $2, while a store down the block charges 50¢ for the same size soda and $1.50 for a better burger.

Exercise 3. Write the sentences in the order you numbered them to form a paper describing an unappealing school cafeteria.

Exercise 4. Write a paper about a good cafeteria. You may use the paper from exercise 3 as a model by changing bad characteristics to good ones. For instance, you can change long lines and bad service to short lines and quick, friendly service. Or you can use your own words and experiences.

SET 8. STEEL DRUMS FROM STRIKING HANDS

The sounds, sights, and impressions that a writer experienced as she became acquainted with steel drums and fascinated by the skillful power of a drum maker's hands are described in the following exercise.

Exercise 1. Number the sentences within each paragraph to form the best logical order.

Vocabulary
lilt: speak rhythmically with fluctuating pitch.

I

_____ Following the music to its source led us to the pool deck of one of the hotels and a man playing a set of double tenor steel drums.

_____ Last year my husband and I were walking on the beach when we heard something that sounded like a xylophone or a piano but even more pleasant than either.

_____ I watched my husband's fascination grow as he engaged the musician in a conversation that led to inviting him, Walter, and his drums to our house that evening.

II

_____ George is a pan maker, and my husband decided to call him and order a set.

_____ It was then that we learned about George Richards, Walter's lifelong friend from his native Granada who now lives about 60 miles from our house.

_____ When he came, he explained that steel drums, or pans as they are called by those who play them, are handmade from 55 gallon steel oil cans and cannot be purchased at any department or music store.

III

_____ However, he understood that we wanted a set of steel drums as soon as possible.

_____ His words, bathed in a rich Caribbean accent, were carried by a voice so soft that they were almost lost in the lilting island tones.

_____ Talking with George on the telephone was difficult.

_____ And it was only 2 days plus a few hours past our scheduled meeting that he arrived at our house with a, "Hello, Mon. I made your drum."

IV

_____ A knit cap was pulled over his small ears and down to his neat eyebrows that framed large, sensitive brown eyes which almost squinted shut when he flashed his wide grin.

_____ He was dressed in an army-styled green coat that hung on his long, lanky frame to the middle of the calves of his legs.

_____ His teeth were in straight rows and seemed even whiter against his dark skin and short, black beard and mustache.

V

_2_ His neatly shaved, brown head hovered somewhere near the ceiling as he explained that he had to "find the notes in the pans."

_____ After the drums were set up in the house, George removed his coat and hat.

_____ He then borrowed our ball-peen hammer to tune the drums.

_____ Smoke encircled the whole scene as he puffed constantly on his Kool cigarette.

_4_ Bent at the waist with his right ear close to the pan, he began to strike each note until it sounded as he thought it should.

_____ Occasionally the end of the cigarette would fall into the pans, but his concentration never faltered as the ashes danced to the vibrations.

VI

_____ As he tuned the drums, I noticed his wide hands that seemed too big to be carried even by his muscular arms.

_____ After every other strike of the hammer he would force each note smooth with the tips of the long, brawny fingers of his left hand.

__4__ While I watched this process, I was amazed at the strength and genius his hands represented.

__2__ He struck the metal over and over again with the hammer held so tightly in his right hand that his dark skin paled at the knuckles as the bones pushed against his taut flesh.

VII

_____ I went back into the house when I heard him begin to play chords.

_____ The pounding of the hammer finally drove me outdoors.

_____ He greeted me with, "See, I made you good pans."

_____ I do not know how George stood the noise, but he didn't stop until each of the 30 notes sounded as they should.

VIII

_____ It was then that I understood why our telephone conversations were so difficult to understand: I needed to see his hands; they made everything clear.

_____ Every word was expressed with a gesture that accented its meaning.

_____ When we talked about music and his life on Granada, my attention was again drawn to his hands.

_____ I realized that just as they held the secret to making the pans, they also held the key to understanding his verbal communication.

IX

_____ Several times we have given the call, and he has returned, maybe not just when expected because he travels to various parts of the country "touching up" drums that he has made.

_____ Before George left that night he promised to come back whenever the drums needed tuning.

_____ However, he eventually gets back to us, and we are always glad for the chance to once again observe his magic hands at work.

_____ "Just give me a call, Mon. I'll get back to you," he promised.

Exercise 2. Write the sentences in the order you numbered them to form a paper describing sounds, sights, and impressions experienced in becoming acquainted with steel drums and George the drum maker.

Analysis Of Description Papers

The exercises in this unit illustrated how word pictures can be painted of people and situations. In writing descriptions, remember that *describe* means tell about something in detail. Your reader will only see, hear, and feel the experiences you are describing if you present enough details for him to recreate the experiences in his own mind. Without these details, he is left staring at a blank screen.

Exercise sets 6 and 8 showed how a description can take the form of a comparison with something familiar. In set 8 the sound of steel drums was conveyed by comparing it to the sound of a piano or xylophone. Set 6 portrayed the structure of a tiny wheat kernel by comparing it part-by-part to the structure of an egg. Such comparisons provide the reader with a link between the unknown and the known.

Try to be systematic in your descriptions. For the buffet table (set 3), the description began at the far right with the plates and progressed systematically until the silverware was reached at the far left. The cafeteria description began with the short hours, then followed a path through the serving line, past the food, and into the dining area. The description of the wheat kernel was introduced with the statement, "An egg has three parts: shell, white, and yolk." Then the description of the kernel followed the same order: bran, endosperm, and germ. Being systematic like this makes it much easier for a reader to follow and visualize your description.

Finally, when you are looking for the right word to convey some impression, you might find a thesaurus handy. A thesaurus is a book listing synonyms (words of similar meaning) and antonyms (opposite meaning). This special type of dictionary can lead you to just the word for making a description vivid. If you do not own a thesaurus, you can buy one reasonably at a paperback bookstore.

Independent Writing

Exercises for writing your own, original descriptions will be given in the next unit, after a brief discussion of how writers actually write.

Unit

3

The Writing Process

In the last unit you numbered sentences and wrote them into papers. But it is important to understand that the authors of this book were not able to just sit down and write these papers in their final form the way you did. Instead, like most other writers, they went through a series of stages.

First, writers get a general idea about a topic. Bringing to mind related facts and examples, they talk to themselves as if they were telling someone else everything they consider important on the subject. They do research in encyclopedias or other reference sources if additional information is needed. And they may brainstorm to bring many ideas to mind quickly (brainstorming is discussed later).

Writers organize their ideas mentally and generally find it useful to write a rough outline, emphasizing major points and examples. As writers talk to themselves in outlining a paper, they may try to think of good sentences to introduce or explain ideas. When a good sentence comes to mind, it is written down immediately so it will not be forgotten (most writers know that thinking up good sentences is hard work). Sometimes entire paragraphs are written this way and saved for later use in the paper.

Then writers begin their actual papers. Often new ideas come to mind as they write, and these are added to the ideas already in the outline. After writing several sentences or paragraphs, writers generally stop to read over their material. Quite frequently they see better ways to express ideas, so they scratch out phrases or sentences and re-write them. Gradually writers work through all the ideas in the outline until the paper is completed.

But experienced writers know they are still not done. This is just the first draft. Writers have found that when they read a paper that they have written just once, they almost always discover ways to revise and improve it. Of course spelling and grammar errors are corrected. But the most important reason for revising is to express meaning more clearly. A writer may discover that his or her meaning is vague at certain points, or that he or she has not fully explained relationships between ideas. Often such lack of clarity is seen only after a paper has been completed, and the writer reads it from start to finish with a fresh eye.

A second purpose for revising is to improve word choice. Frequently, in reading through a completed paper, the writer thinks of better words to use. The writer might change "very large" to "gigantic" or "umpire in the game of baseball" to "baseball umpire." He or she looks for places where more powerful words or compact phrases can be used.

A third purpose for revising is to improve sentence structure. A writer might find that he or she has written one short sentence after another, with no long sentences to change the pace. Or the writer might find he or she has started five sentences in a row with "The . . . ," giving an immature, boring quality to the writing. Such problems are corrected by rewriting several sentences so they don't all start the same way or have the same length.

A fourth purpose for revising is that as a writer reads through the first draft, he or she often thinks of new ideas or illustrations to enrich the paper. Many writers report that their papers continue to improve as they reread and revise them three and even four times. Revising is an important part of writing. With your own writing it is to your advantage to never submit a paper to a teacher or boss without first reading it through, correcting spelling or grammar errors, and revising wherever necessary.

In summary, writing a paper generally involves these stages:

1. Thinking of ideas: talking to yourself about the topic as if you were explaining it to someone else; perhaps doing research in encyclopedias, etc; perhaps brainstorming to get many ideas quickly.

2. Organizing ideas: making an outline; thinking of sentences to introduce and express ideas.

3. Writing a first draft.

4. Revising: correcting spelling and grammar errors; expressing ideas more clearly; using more powerful language; improving sentences; adding ideas.

5. Revising again—preferably after not reading the paper for at least a day: fresh ideas come to mind for explaining and expressing thoughts; awkward or unclear sections may only be recognized after a time lapse.

The first exercise below asks you to describe a wall with things on it. You will not need to think of ideas or examples to write about. But you will have to organize the description systematically and formulate sentences that clearly describe the shapes and positions of the objects. After writing the first draft, read it over carefully. Of course, correct spelling and grammar errors. In addition, you will probably find sentences that can be revised to make them sound better or describe the objects more clearly.

The second exercise asks you to describe yourself. This requires thinking of the characteristics you want to describe, organizing the description, and finding the right words to express your thoughts. Because this is a more difficult writing task, you can expect to do more revising before you have a well-written description of yourself.

Independent Writing (Description)

1. Describe the wall shown below. Rather than moving from one end to the other, as in the buffet table paper, you might start at the door and first move to the left, then to the right. Remember to describe the shapes of things with words like triangular and arched-shaped.

   After writing a first draft, read it over to correct spelling/grammar errors and also to describe the wall more clearly.

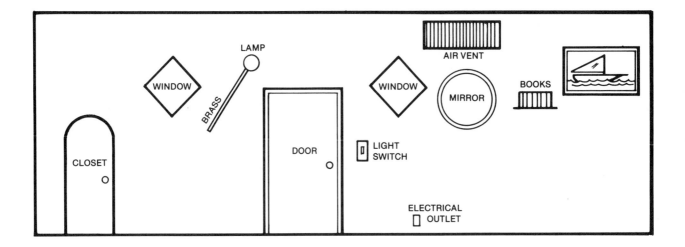

2. Write a description of yourself in a minimum of 150 words. Include physical characteristics such as overall size and body type along with details about eye and hair color, hair style, etc. Also describe what you are now wearing, with details about clothes color, design, etc. After writing a first draft, read it over to improve the description of yourself in any way possible and also to correct spelling/grammar errors.

3. Write a 150-word description of the room you are in right now. Include furniture and objects on walls.

4. Pick one of the following topics to write on.

   a. Assume you have unlimited funds to design an automobile. Write a 200-word description of your ideal car, including details like body style, color, seats, dashboard, sound system, engine, and other equipment.

   You might begin by brainstorming: Think of everything you could possibly want in or on a car.

   b. Assume you have unlimited funds to design your own living room (or bedroom). Write a 200-word description of your ideal living room (or bedroom), including details such as view, shape, walls, rug, furniture, lighting, mirrors, electronic equipment, etc.

   You might begin by brainstorming: Let your imagination run wild. List lots of wall colors, window styles, views, wallpaper designs, furniture, everything that comes to mind. You might get additional ideas by recalling beautiful rooms you have visited or seen in magazines and movies.

5. Why did you (may you) choose a certain career? Write a 100-word description of that career in terms of two or three characteristics important to you. Here are examples of job characteristics people consider: type of work, salary, working conditions, hours, training or educational requirements, chance for advancement, vacations, travel, job security. Write a detailed description of two or three such characteristics for your career.

Unit

4

Describing A Sequence of Actions or Events

Writing often takes the form of describing a series of actions or events. One example is a history textbook, which recounts the events considered important during some time period. Another example is a description of the events occurring on a trip, or over the course of a day, or even during a fight between two angry cats.

Sometimes in describing a series of events you say that one event caused another one. History books, for example, devote much space and thought to tracing the causes of major wars. At times you may show how one event caused a second event that, in turn, had still another effect, forming a cause–effect chain. Several writing patterns for presenting cause–effect relations are illustrated in the exercises.

Another type of paper that relates a series of actions is called a process paper. A process paper describes how something is accomplished, such as the process of passing a federal law in the United States. Somewhat similar to the process paper is the instructions paper, which tells the reader how he or she can do something like make a pancake or operate a VCR. An instructions paper is generally more detailed than a process paper because its purpose is to allow the reader to perform every step him or herself.

All the papers in this unit share the common element that they describe actions or events occurring over time. Descriptions of events occurring over time often use terms like <u>before</u>, <u>after</u>, <u>two hours later</u>, <u>in 1865</u>, <u>first</u>, <u>second</u>, <u>next</u>, <u>then</u>, and <u>finally</u>. Cause–effect descriptions use <u>because</u>, <u>since</u>, <u>therefore</u>, <u>so</u>, <u>consequently</u>, and <u>result</u>. Note how such terms connect ideas and paragraphs in the papers that follow so you can use them in your own writing.

Writing For Learning

Many of the following exercises ask you to write sentences in the best logical order. To obtain the greatest benefit, do not copy the words letter-by-letter. Instead, use these steps for each sentence.

1. Read as many words as you believe you can write correctly from memory (usually five to 10 words).

2. Write those words from memory, including all capitals and punctuation marks.

3. Check back to the original sentence and correct any errors you made.

4. Read the next group of words and repeat the above steps.

Generally you will be able to read, memorize, and correctly write between five and 10 words. Sometimes you may be able to remember an entire simple sentence correctly. But with a large, difficult-to-spell word, you may only try to write that one word correctly from memory. Writing from memory will make you more aware of the spelling, grammar, punctuation, and word patterns used in standard written English.

Section 1   Cause–Effect

When one event precedes another, we sometimes conclude that the first event causes the second. If a person has several drinks in a bar and then drives his or her car into a telephone pole, we may conclude that excessive drinking caused the accident. Of course, we cannot always say that one event causes another just because the first event regularly precedes the second. The 8:00 a.m. train precedes the 8:10 train every morning, but we do not say that the arrival of the 8:00 a.m. train causes the arrival of the later one. However, the exercises in this section are about events with cause–effect relations.

In unit 1, section 7 you wrote sentences expressing cause–effect relationships like this.

Cause: Brian fell asleep smoking.
Effect: The bed caught fire.

Combined: The bed caught fire because Brian fell asleep smoking.
or
Because Brian fell asleep smoking, the bed caught fire.

In this section you will analyze and write longer cause–effect descriptions.

Set 1. A Chain Of Causes

Sometimes an action or situation has an effect that is itself the cause of another effect. This is called a cause–effect chain and is illustrated in the following exercises.

Exercise 1. Number these sentences so they start with a cause and then explain how this led to an effect on the social security system.

Vocabulary

bankrupt: having no money, out of business
consequently: as a result
fatal: causing death

_____ Consequently, people are living longer and the proportion of the population over 65 has increased.

_____ Medicine has recently conquered many diseases that used to be fatal.

_____ Because there are now relatively more elderly retirees taking money out of the social security system and fewer working-age people paying into it, the system is threatened with bankruptcy.

Exercise 2. Write the sentences in the order you numbered them to form a paragraph describing a cause–effect chain.

Exercise 3. The paragraph you just wrote described a cause–effect chain. Here is the beginning of the chain.

Relationship 1.

Cause: Medicine has recently conquered many diseases that used to be fatal.

Effect: People are living longer and the proportion of the population over 65 has increased.

Relationship 2.

Cause: The proportion of the population over 65 has increased.

Effect: Relatively fewer people are putting money into and more are taking money out of the social security system.

Relationship 3.

Cause: _____

Effect: _____

Notice that the effect in relationship 1 is the cause in relationship 2. Use complete sentences to fill in the cause and effect for relationship 3.

Exercise 4. The paragraph you wrote in exercise 2 began with a cause and ended with an effect. But sometimes you may begin with the effect and then explain its causes. Number the following sentences so they start with the effect and then explain the causes.

_____ The result is relatively fewer working-age people paying into the social security system and more elderly retirees taking money out, which is financially unhealthy.

_____ The social security system is threatened with bankruptcy, partly because of progress in medicine.

_____ Consequently, people are living longer and the proportion of the population over 65 is increasing.

_____ Medical science has recently conquered many diseases that used to be fatal.

Exercise 5. Write the sentences in the order you numbered them to form a paragraph describing an effect and its causes.

SET 2. MULTIPLE CAUSES

Sometimes several causes contribute to an effect. For example, excessive speed combined with wet roads might have caused an automobile accident. Another example is shown in these exercises.

Exercise 1. The following sentences describe an unfortunate situation and three causes contributing to it. Number the sentences in the best logical order.

Vocabulary

mobile: moving often, able to move.

_____ Finally, because of increased real estate and heating costs, houses and apartments have become smaller.

_____ First, the majority of working-age American women hold jobs, so they don't have time to care for an aged parent.

_____ In earlier times, and still in places such as China, the elderly were cared for in the families of their grown children.

_____ Second, American families are highly mobile, moving frequently to obtain better jobs or other benefits.

_____ But this is no longer the case in America for several reasons.

_____ There is no longer an extra room for grandma.

_____ This divides families by hundreds or even thousands of miles, rather than leaving adult children near their elderly parents.

Exercise 2. Write the sentences in the order you numbered them to form a paragraph stating a problem and three causes.

Exercise 3. The paragraph you just wrote presented three reasons (causes) why the elderly are not being cared for by their grown children. But the paragraph also explained causes behind these three causes. For example, the first cause given was that American women don't have time to care for aged parents. But this was said to result from something else. State in a complete sentence why American women don't have time.

Cause: _____

Exercise 4. State in a complete sentence why families are divided by great distances.

Cause: _____

Exercise 5. State in a complete sentence why there is no longer an extra room for grandma.

Cause: _____

Exercise 6. The chart below is one way to clearly show the cause–effect relationships presented in the paragraph. Several causes and effects already have been written in the chart. Write the missing entries in the spaces provided. Note that Cause 3 has two parts.

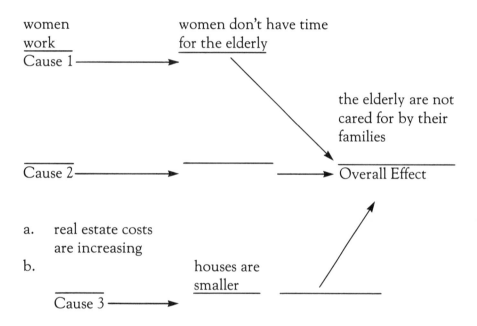

women
work
Cause 1

women don't have time
for the elderly

the elderly are not
cared for by their
families

Cause 2

Overall Effect

a.   real estate costs
     are increasing
b.

Cause 3

houses are
smaller

SET 3. ACTION WITH BOTH BAD AND GOOD EFFECTS

Sometimes an action with intended good effects also has bad effects. Among the following sentences, one describes a government action, another describes a negative effect of the action, and the remainder explain the positive effect.

Exercise 1. Number the following sentences to first describe a government action, then a negative effect, and finally the positive effect.

_____ But the special caps save lives.

_____ Several years ago the government passed a law requiring drug bottles to have child-proof caps.

_____ By keeping toddlers out of such mischief, child-proof caps have prevented thousands of hospital visits and deaths.

_____ Toddlers think pills are candy and try to gulp them down while mommy is loading the washing machine.

_____ Some people got mad and argued with pharmacists because they had trouble opening the bottles.

Exercise 2. Write the sentences to form a paragraph that begins with a government action, then describes a negative result of the action, and finally the positive result.

Exercise 3. With all material from the exercises just given out of sight, write a paragraph about any government action that had both negative and positive results. You may write about child-proof caps, but be sure all material from the exercises is away.

SET 4. "SURE, DEAR"

Do people listen when you talk? The following sentences can be arranged to describe how one person caused another to stop listening.

Exercise 1. Number the sentences to form the best logical order.

_____ Without looking up from his paper, he replied automatically, "Yes, dear. Thank you, dear."

_____ Serving him some pancakes, she said, "Have several. I filled them with cockroaches."

_____ She barely heard her husband when he asked for another piece of toast or something.

_____ A woman decided to test whether her husband heard anything she said when he had his head buried in the paper during breakfast.

_____ She just replied, "Sure, dear," and read on.

_____ So she sat down with the editorial page and began enjoying a humorous article about the city's mayor.

Exercise 2. Write the sentences in the order you numbered them.

Exercise 3. With all material from exercises 1 and 2 out of sight, write a paragraph telling (as best you remember it) the same "Sure dear" story just told.

SET 5.

The following sentences can be arranged into a paper describing some dangerous cause–effect relationships.

Exercise 1. Number the sentences within each paragraph to form the best logical order.

I

_____ The tobacco industry responded to these findings by marketing filter cigarettes advertised as lower in tar and nicotine.

_____ There are several reasons for this.

__2__ The tar in cigarettes was identified as the substance producing cancer, while the nicotine was found harmful to the heart and also addictive (causing a person to crave more cigarettes).

_____ But recent studies reveal that "low tar and nicotine" cigarettes have not reduced the risk of cancer and heart disease.

_____ Around 1960 it was established that smoking cigarettes increased a person's chance of developing cancer and heart disease.

II

_____ While both of these flavorings are safe to eat, they can cause cancer when smoked.

_____ First, it has been discovered that other substances in cigarettes besides tar and nicotine are also health hazards when they are burned and inhaled.

_____ Simply eliminating the two flavorings would not solve the problem because there are about 2,000 other chemicals (such as dangerous carbon monoxide) which are produced by a burning cigarette.

_____ For example, cigarette manufacturers add licorice and sugar to improve the flavor of cigarettes.

III

_____ For example, he may inhale more deeply and hold the smoke longer.

_____ Through this misunderstanding, he will inhale a greater amount of other dangerous chemicals than he would by smoking a smaller number of regular cigarettes.

_____ Or he may smoke more cigarettes per day, believing that "low tar and nicotine" cigarettes are safe and can be smoked in large quantity without risk.

_____ A second reason is that once a person is addicted to nicotine, he finds ways to obtain the amount of nicotine his body craves, even with low nicotine cigarettes.

IV

_____ In fact, a report in the medical journal *Lancet* stated that the risk of heart attack was just as high for a group of filter-cigarette smokers as for regular-cigarette smokers.

_____ To stamp out the cancer and heart disease still being caused by smoking, people must be made aware of these dangers.

_____ For these and other reasons, it is now believed that no cigarettes are safe.

Exercise 2. Write the sentences in the order you numbered them to form a paper explaining some of the cause–effect relationships that make low tar and nicotine cigarettes unsafe.

Section 2   Describing A Process and Giving Instructions

A great deal of practical writing takes the form of explaining how something is done – or telling the reader exactly how he or she can do something. In this section the first set of exercises involves a brief, general description of the law-making process. From reading this description a person gets an overview of how laws are made, although the selection does not present enough details for a person to actually go through all the steps of making a law. By contrast, the second set of exercises involves instructions for baking cornbread that are detailed enough to allow you to bake this special bread for dinner tonight. When you do Set 2, notice how the instructions present every step in order. Poor instructions sometimes confuse people by jumping back and forth among the steps.

SET 1. DESCRIBING A PROCESS: LAW-MAKING

> Vocabulary
> bill: draft (rough copy) of a proposed law
> Congress: Senate and House of Representatives
> majority: more than half
> modifications: changes
> veto: a "no" vote

Exercise 1. Number the following sentences in the best logical order.

_____ If the committee approves the bill (often only with modifications), it is presented to the entire House and Senate for a vote.

_____ Making a new federal law applying to the entire United States requires a number of steps.

_____ First a Senator or member of the House of Representatives introduces a bill, which is assigned to a committee (e.g., Labor Committee) for study and discussion.

_____ The bill must receive a majority of the votes in both the House and Senate in order to be passed on to the President for his signature or veto.

_____ However, if he casts a veto, the bill generally dies.

_____ If the President signs it, then it becomes a law for the whole country.

_____ A bill vetoed by the President could still become a law, but it would have to return to Congress and receive a two-thirds favorable vote, so this occurs infrequently.

Exercise 2. Write the sentences in the order you numbered them to describe the process of making a new federal law.

SET 2. GRANNY'S CORNBREAD

Good cooks have secrets that make their dishes especially delicious. If you want to prepare one of their specialties, you must follow their procedure exactly. Here is an example.

Exercise 1. Number the sentences within each paragraph to form the best logical order.

Vocabulary
staple: a basic food like sugar or butter.

I

_____ The magic lay in knowing exactly how Granny used those simple ingredients.

_____ Many people "stopped by" around supper time just to watch her make this special bread because they had learned from their own failures that only knowing the ingredients was not enough.

_____ When my grandmother was alive, she was one of the best cooks in our county and famous for baking that old-time staple, cornbread.

II

_____ She said you couldn't use just any pan to bake cornbread with such a crispy, golden-brown crust that it flipped onto a plate without leaving even a crumb behind.

_____ Granny's first secret was her "seasoned" 10-inch iron skillet.

_____ Using an unseasoned pan resulted in clumps of cornbread sticking to the sides, according to Granny.

_____ This seasoning process was repeated three times before the skillet became "the skillet" for baking cornbread; it was never used for anything else, and it was never washed.

_____ Then she put it away until the next day when she again rubbed it with grease and baked it in the oven.

_____ To season her iron skillet, Granny had (several years earlier) rubbed grease onto the inside and outside of the skillet and put it into a hot (400 degrees) oven to bake for 15 minutes.

III

_____ At the same time, she greased the inside of the skillet and put it on a stove burner set for low heat so the skillet would be smokey-hot when the cornbread batter was poured in later.

_____ In actually making the cornbread, Granny first preheated the oven to 450 degrees.

_____ The remaining steps were simple, but if they weren't followed in sequence, the cornbread would turn lumpy or rise unevenly in the skillet.

_____ This dry mixture was stirred together by hand for about 2 minutes to make sure everything was mixed evenly.

_____ Into a large bowl Granny put 1 cup of flour, 1 cup of cornmeal, 1 teaspoon of sugar, ½ teaspoon of salt, and 4 teaspoons of baking powder.

_____ Finally, 1 cup of buttermilk was stirred into the batter to make it moist and to give the cornbread its rich taste.

IV

_____ When the timer rang, Granny took the skillet from the oven and pressed a plate to the top of it, flipped them over, and lifted off the skillet to reveal a golden, delicious-smelling cake of cornbread.

_____ The batter was poured into the slightly smoking skillet, which was then placed in the hot oven for 20 minutes.

Exercise 2. Write the sentences in the order you numbered them to form a description of the procedure Granny used to make cornbread.

Exercise 3. Rewrite the procedure for baking Granny's cornbread as instructions to the reader rather than a description of Granny's activities. Tell the reader what he or she should do. You could start like this:

To bake great cornbread you must first have a "seasoned" skillet. Rub grease on the inside and outside of a 10-inch iron skillet. Then put it into a hot. . . .

Section 3   Narrating A Series Of Events

The remaining exercises in this unit illustrate some of the language and logic that may be used in describing any series of events: historical or personal.

SET 1. WORDS SHOWING SEQUENCE

In writing a paper about a series of actions you often use words like <u>first</u>, <u>next</u>, and <u>after</u> to show sequence or order. Following are six such words used in tieing together sentences describing a series of actions. Use each word only once in filling the blanks for the paragraph that follows.

Next   At   Then   When   After   First

My alarm wakes me every weekday at 7:00 a.m. _____ I shower and shave. _____ I select my clothes for the day and get dressed. _____ I eat breakfast. _____ breakfast I read the paper. _____ my dad is ready, I leave with him for school. _____ 8:30 I begin classes.

SET 2. VARY YOUR SENTENCE PATTERNS

If every sentence in a history paper began: "In 1783 . . . ," "In 1803 . . . ," "In 1819 . . ." — the paper would seem immature and dull. One way to vary such sentences is to change the position where you give the date. The date can be placed near the beginning, near the middle, or near the end of a sentence.

Example 1

Date Near Beginning	In 1819 Florida was purchased from Spain.
Date Near Middle	Florida was purchased in 1819 from Spain.
Date Near End	Florida was purchased from Spain in 1819.

Another way to give the date of an event is to tell how many years it occurred after another event, as shown in example 2.

Example 2.

| Dull ——— | In 1980 Reagan was elected president. |
| | In 1984 Reagan was again elected president. |

| Better ——— | In 1980 Reagan was elected president. |
| | Four years later Reagan was again elected president. |

Use these sentence patterns in the following exercise.

Exercise 1. Following are six sentences all beginning with a date. Rewrite them as a paragraph with varying sentence patterns. Let the first sentence and only one other sentence have the date at the beginning. For the others, have at least one sentence with the date near the middle, at least one with the date near the end, and one with the date given as the number of years following another date.

In 1776 the 13 original colonies declared their independence from Britain and became the United States.

In 1783 the U.S. obtained most of the territory between the Appalachian Mountains and the Mississippi River through a treaty with Britain.

In 1803 Napoleon sold the Louisiana territory to the U.S. for $15 million.

In 1819 Florida was purchased from Spain.

In 1845 the citizens of Texas (at the time a separate country) voted to join the United States.

In 1853 additional land in the Southwest was acquired through the Gadsden Purchase.

SET 3. THE PRACTICAL UNJOKER

The following sentences can be arranged into a story relating several humorous incidents.

Exercise 1. Number the sentences in the best logical order.

_____ But Uncle Fred just turned on the lamp switch and began reading his paper in the dark as if nothing was wrong.

_____ That is, until we spent a week visiting our Uncle Fred at his ranch.

_____ When my sister and I were kids, we loved playing practical jokes.

_____ On the first evening we took the bulb out of the lamp by his chair.

_____ Then he sprinkled some on our corn flakes and told us to eat all of our cereal if we wanted to go horseback riding with him later.

_____ When Uncle Fred came to breakfast he sprinkled two spoons of it on his corn flakes and began eating without blinking an eye.

_____ We were surprised but not crushed, so the next morning we tiptoed into the kitchen before Uncle Fred and filled the sugar bowl with salt.

_____ Uncle Fred received a phone call just as he began making egg salad sandwiches for our lunch.

_____ We tried just one more trick.

_____ By the time we finished those sandwiches, we had our fill of practical jokes.

_____ When Uncle Fred came back, he cracked the eggs into a bowl and, as if nothing unusual had happened, he stirred in a spoonful of mayonnaise.

_____ With his back turned, we substituted uncooked eggs for the hard boiled ones he had placed on the table.

_____ Then he spread the slimy mixture onto some bread, served us the "egg salad" sandwiches, and watched while we ate them.

Exercise 2. Write the sentences in the order you numbered them. You may divide the sentences into two or three paragraphs if you prefer.

SET 4. SMOKING ADDICTION

The following sentences can be arranged to describe a series of events marking the ruin of a famous person's health by smoking addiction.

Exercise 1. Number the sentences in the best logical order.

Vocabulary
psychiatry: branch of medicine specializing in mental illness.

_____ His first danger signal was the development of an irregular heartbeat accompanied by severe chest pains whenever he smoked.

_____ Freud smoked about 20 cigars a day.

_____ An illustration of how severe an addiction to tobacco can become is seen in the tragic life of Sigmund Freud, the father of modern psychiatry.

_____ The chest pains caused him to swear off cigars temporarily, but shortly he began smoking one a day, then two, and gradually built back up to his full-scale addiction.

_____ Next Freud developed cancer of the mouth.

_____ But soon he resumed, describing his craving as "the torture being beyond human power to bear."

_____ On the advice of a physician he stopped smoking for a while to halt the cancer.

_____ But still Freud smoked, until the cancer finally took his life.

__8__ The consequence was 33 jaw operations over 16 years, ending with Freud's jaw being totally removed and replaced by a painful mechanical jaw.

Exercise 2. Write the sentences in the order you numbered them to form a description of how smoking addiction ruined Freud's health.

SET 5. RAW RAGE

Can you recall and describe a series of events leading to an incident that left you shocked, injured, and forever more cautious? The following sentences can be arranged to tell such a story.

Exercise 1. Number the sentences within each paragraph so they sound best to you. You may discover more than one good arrangement for some paragraphs.

Vocabulary
agony: intense pain of mind or body.
anguish: intense pain, especially of mind.
confrontation: face-to-face meeting of enemies.
deter: stop, delay.
instincts: inborn drives
minor: unimportant.
momentary: lasting just a moment.
temporarily: for a short period of time.

I

_____ After almost 12 years of treating this animal as if he were a child—caring for him during his illnesses, providing him with the best of food, holding him for countless hours, and loving him as a faithful companion—he bit me as if I were a total stranger.

_____ Although it was not as serious as a disease or a life-threatening accident, it has caused me much physical pain and mental anguish.

_____ My cat bit me.

_____ Last summer I had a painful, scarring experience.

II

_____ I admit that I was not blameless in the incident.

_____ He was involved in a fight with another cat.

_____ And I had been warned many times about the consequences of interfering in such a confrontation.

_____ By the time I arrived they were fighting and rolling on a neighbor's porch like characters out of a western movie.

_____ Nevertheless, at the first howls of battle, I went to rescue him.

_____ My screams to stop were ignored; they continued to fight.

_____ Even falling from the porch onto hard concrete did not deter them for a moment.

III

_____ I followed them across the street as they chased each other under and between parked cars.

_____ Eventually they came to a momentary standoff under a red van.

_____ As I tried to coax my cat out, the other cat broke his stance and ran into the underbrush of a neighboring yard.

_____ My cat followed, but suddenly, as if bored by the whole thing, he returned to where I was standing.

_____ He purred and rubbed against my leg.

_____ Then I picked him up and headed toward home.

_____ I bent down and patted him affectionately, noting scratches on his ears and nose that would soon be scars for life.

_____ I tried to drop him, but I moved too slowly.

_____ All at once his body stiffened and a threatening growl came from deep inside his throat.

_____ Then I felt his fangs puncture my flesh and sink deeper and deeper until they struck a bone.

_____ He twisted around in my arms, and I felt his mouth close around my wrist.

IV

_____ When he finally let go, blood flowed down the front and back of my hand as it began swelling to twice its normal size.

_____ It throbbed with pain; only thoughts of the need to clean the wounds got me to my feet again.

_____ Fourteen pounds of unleashed fury hung from my wrist.

_____ I fell to my knees and slung my arm, trying to get him to release me.

V

__3_ I still could not believe that my cat had attacked me so viciously.

_____ The pain was constant, but that was minor compared to the mental agony I was suffering.

_____ For 3 days my wrist and palm were so swollen that I could not open or close my hand.

_____ Those other owners probably held the same belief, until their pets reacted to instincts temporarily blinded and out of control.

_____ I had heard horror stories about other animals attacking their owners, but I had been sure that our relationship was different, stronger.

VI

_____ Oh, I still pat him, feed him, let him sit at my feet, but I do not pick him up and hold him in my arms—not yet.

_____ Today my wrist has four puncture scars that will be there forever.

_____ Of that part I remain very fearful.

_____ The scars on our relationship are also permanent.

_____ I still love him, but I do not trust that part of his being that denied the existence of our relationship.

Exercise 2. Write the sentences in the order you numbered them to form a story about a series of events that left the writer with a lingering fear of animals.

Analysis Of Papers Describing A Series Of Events Or Actions

Section 1 illustrated descriptions of cause–effect relationships. A writer may first describe a cause and then the effect it produced, or the effect may be described first and then its causes (set 1). If several causes contributed to an effect, these can be systematically described (set 2). And when one event causes a second event which, in turn, has still another effect, the entire cause–effect chain can be described (set 1).

Section 2 showed how to describe a process or give a series of instructions. Set 1 involved a brief description of the law-making process. Obviously this was not intended to be detailed instructions for the reader to follow. It only provided an overall picture of how a federal law is made.

Set 2 was different. It described Granny's cornbread-making process in enough detail that a person with a little kitchen experience could actually bake the delicious treat for dinner. In exercise 3 you were asked to rewrite the description of Granny's activities as direct instructions for a reader. Think of how many types of instructions you see regularly. Every appliance and machine you buy—from a hair dryer to an automobile—comes with operating instructions. Instructions also are found in cookbooks, tax forms, home repair manuals—the list is endless. People were paid to write all of these instructions, so you can see that the ability to write clear instructions is valuable. The key to writing good instructions is describing every step the reader must take, from first to last. Remember that you will not be there to explain anything. Describe the steps in the correct order and in a form that can be easily understood.

Generally the sentences used for instructions are grammatically different than most sentences because they do not contain a subject. Compare these two sentences.

Granny greased the inside of a pan.
↑   ↑
Subject   Verb

Grease the inside of a pan.
↑   ↑
No Subject   Verb

In the first sentence the subject is "Granny." The second sentence does not actually contain a subject, although the implied subject is "you." If the implied subject (you) was included, the sentence would look like this.

You grease the inside of a pan.
↑   ↑
Subject   Verb

In writing instructions, the word "you" is only included occasionally and sometimes not at all. Notice in the following three sentences that "you" is included only in the opening sentence.

First you should buckle your seatbelt. Then check that the transmission lever is in neutral or park. Place the square key into the ignition switch on the steering post and turn to the "start" position.

The word "you" could also be deleted from the opening sentence like this: First buckle your seatbelt.

The street directions that you wrote in set 1 of unit 2 were a form of instructions. As you can see from that example, along with the Cornbread exercise and the excerpt from an automobile operator's manual, the sentences used in instructions are generally simple and direct. Whenever you read a set of instructions, pay special attention to the writing style so that you too can write clear instructions for others to follow.

The last section of exercises illustrated patterns for describing any series of events. Whenever you tell a story about things that happened to you or someone else, you are describing a series of events. With practice you can develop skill writing such descriptions in personal letters, short stories, and perhaps someday even a best-selling novel. Read short stories, biographies, and novels to see the language and patterns employed by successful writers, and then practice using similar techniques in your own writing.

Independent Writing

In doing the following assignments, remember that good writers generally read through and revise a paper TWO or THREE times before considering it finished. After you write a first draft, read it from the beginning and revise sentences which can be expressed more clearly or smoothly. Also add any new ideas and examples that you can think of. REWRITE THE WHOLE PAPER IF NECESSARY. Finally, read your paper once more to catch spelling and grammar errors. This is the only way to write well.

1. Write instructions that will teach a friend how to play your favorite game.

   Or,

   Write instructions telling a friend how to change a tire, fry an egg, make a pancake, or do any other such task.

   You might begin by making a list of all the equipment used and every step taken. Then organize the steps into the correct sequence from first to last. Take the time to include enough details about the steps so that the reader understands your instructions. After writing the first draft, read it through, correct spelling/grammar errors, and revise it wherever necessary to make the instructions more clear. If possible, give it to a classmate to read, and rewrite any portion of the instructions that is unclear.

2. Describe (minimum 150 words) a series of actions you took (like driving to school) or events you experienced or witnessed today. This might have occurred before you left home, while traveling somewhere, at a restaurant, etc. If any cause–effect relationships were involved, describe them fully.

If you have trouble thinking of something to write about, try brainstorming for 1 minute. Brainstorming means letting as many ideas as possible come into your mind and writing them down quickly without judging or trying to organize them. Think of everything you did and saw since you woke up this morning and write it all down as it comes to mind. Do not try to write complete sentences. Just get something on paper for each idea so you will not forget it. The beginning of a brainstorming list might look like this:

went to Exxon for gas, self-service pump broken, full-service pump was $1.54 for super unleaded, asked attendant if I could get it for self-service price if I pumped it, no, said company wouldn't allow it, went to Amoco, had trouble with cashier. . . .

After brainstorming for 1 minute, pick some series of actions or events to write about. Do not worry if it is not exciting or funny. Just describe it well for your readers.

3. Write a 100-word paragraph explaining two causes or reasons for one of the following situations.

   a. The air is becoming polluted.
   b. Many Americans are overweight.
   c. Many high school graduates go (do not go) to college.
   d. Many Americans are out of work.
   e. Many women, both single and married, hold jobs.

Begin by describing the situation and one or two examples, such as an example of air pollution. Then describe the two causes, including details or illustrations.

If you have trouble thinking of ideas, try brainstorming. Pick one topic. Then take a full minute to write down all examples, causes or reasons, illustrations of causes, and other ideas that come into your mind.

4. Your instructor may assign additional papers.

Unit

5

Organizing Ideas Into Classification and General–Specific Patterns

This unit presents two of the most widely used patterns for organizing ideas. Part 1 describes Classification and Part 2 covers General–Specific. As you work through the exercises, you may notice that the two patterns are like two sides of a coin. On the surface they look different, but their underlying logic is the same. This is explained more at the end of the unit.

Part 1. Classification

We often group things into categories or classes. This is called <u>classification</u>. For example, food could be classified as American, Chinese, Italian, and so on as shown.

Topic: Food
   Category 1: American
      Example 1: roast beef
      Example 2: corn on the cob

Category 2: Chinese
  Example 1: chow mein
  Example 2: egg foo young
Category 3: Italian
  Example 1: pizza
  Example 2: spaghetti
Category 4: Fench
    etc.

Note that "food" is listed at the top. It is the topic for the classification. Food includes all the things listed below it. Next are the categories of food, such as American and Chinese. Within each category are examples. Try the following sample exercise on classification.

Sample Exercise   The list of things on the left can be organized into the classification pattern shown on the right. Read through the entire list and find the topic that includes everything else. Write it in the space labeled Topic. Then fill in the categories and examples. Complete the exercise before reading the answer.

Hint: Cross out each item on the left as you write it in the outline.

trucks	Topic: _____
trains	Category 1: _____
land transportation vehicles	Example: _____
transportation vehicles	Example: _____
submarines	Example: _____
jet passenger planes	Example: _____
helicopters	Example: _____
canoes	Example: _____
sailboats	Category 2: _____
bicycles	Example: _____
automobiles	Example: _____
air transportation vehicles	Example: _____
ocean liners	Example: _____
spacecraft	Example: _____
motorcycles	Example: _____
small private planes	Category 3: _____
buses	Example: _____
water transportation vehicles	Example: _____
motorboats and motorized yachts	Example: _____
	Example: _____
	Example: _____
	Example: _____

Answer   Transportation vehicles is the broadest term in the list. It includes land transportation vehicles, water transportation vehicles, and air transportation vehicles. So transportation vehicles belongs in the space labeled Topic. The three categories are: land transportation vehicles, water transportation vehicles, and air transportation vehicles. These could be written in any order in the spaces labeled Category 1, 2, and 3. The examples are then listed within the categories. In the answer, the first two categories begin with examples of motorized vehicles and then list nonmotorized vehicles because this is how you might discuss them in a paper—moving from motorized to nonmotorized. The third category has no nonmotorized vehicles because none are widely used for transportation. (You might have added gliders and hot air balloons if you wanted to discuss them in a paper.)

Topic: transportation vehicles

Category 1:   land transportation vehicles

Example: automobiles

Example: motorcycles

Example: trucks

Example: buses

Example: trains

Example: bicycles

Category 2:   water transportation vehicles

Example: ocean liners

Example: motorboats and motorized yachts

Example: submarines

Example: sailboats

Example: canoes

Example: _____

Category 3:   air transportation vehicles

Example: jet passenger planes

Example: helicopters

Example: small private planes

Example: spacecraft

Example: _____

Example: _____

Now begin the exercises.

Exercise 1. Read the list on the left. Then write each item in an appropriate space on the right.

NOTE: Let "other pets" be the last category in the outline.

Hint: Cross out each item on the left as you write it in the outline.

dogs	Topic:_____
Persian cats	Category 1: _____
turtles	Example: _____
other pets	Example: _____
German shepherds	Example: _____
birds	Example: _____
collies	Category 2: _____
canaries	Example: _____
white rats and gerbils	Example: _____
Siamese cats	Example: _____
monkeys	Example: _____
goldfish	Category 3: _____
multi-colored average cats	Example: _____
fish and reptiles	Example: _____
snakes	Example: _____
pets	Example: _____
black cats	Category 4: _____
Siamese fighting fish	Example: _____
parakeets	Example: _____
cocker spaniels	Example: _____
horses	Example: _____
poodles	Category 5: _____
parrots	Example: _____
cats	Example: _____
	Example: _____
	Example: _____

Exercise 2. Notice that the classification outline on the right has two main categories, but one category has two subcategories. Write the items from the list on the left in the appropriate spaces on the right.

Detroit	Topic: _____
major American cities	Category 1: _____
London	Subcategory A: _____
major northern American cities	Example: _____
Tokyo	Example: _____
Chicago	Example: _____
Miami	Example: _____

Dallas	Subcategory B: _____
major cities of the world	Example: _____
major southern American cities	Example: _____
Moscow	Example: _____
Paris	Example: _____
Atlanta	Category 2: _____
Houston	Example: _____
New York	Example: _____
Rome	Example: _____
Peking	Example: _____
major foreign cities	Example: _____
	Example: _____

Exercise 3. For this exercise, notice that the classification outline has two main categories, but the first has two subcategories, whereas the second has three. Write the items from the list on the left in the appropriate spaces on the right.

tables	Topic: _____
dishwashers	Category 1: _____
furniture	Subcategory A: _____
merchandise sold in a store	Example: _____
merchandise for a home	Example: _____
silverware	Example: _____
dining merchandise	Example: _____
plates	Subcategory B: _____
washing machines	Example: _____
skirts	Example: _____
women's clothing	Example: _____
blouses	Example: _____
men's slacks	Category 2: _____
men's clothing	Subcategory A: _____
neckties	Example: _____
sofas	Example: _____
men's suits	Example: _____
clothing	Example: _____
appliances	Subcategory B: _____
desks	Example: _____
chairs	Example: _____
electric irons	Example: _____
drinking glasses	Example: _____
	Subcategory C: _____
	Example: _____
	Example: _____
	Example: _____
	Example: _____

Part 2. General–Specific

One of the most important techniques in effective writing is presenting specific illustrations to support general statements. For example, if you are writing a paper arguing the general point that women are successfully entering traditionally male occupations, you might use women astronauts as one specific illustration. Moreover, in writing about women astronauts, you might use Sally Ride as a specific illustration, describing her experiences to make your ideas concrete. Of course, the terms general and specific are relative, as shown by this diagram.

most general: women successful in traditionally male
            occupations
            women astronauts
most specific: Sally Ride

Forming general–specific relations is important in organizing many papers and is the focus of the following exercises. Try the sample exercise before reading the answer.

Sample Exercise

Instructions: Write the following list in order, with the most general item on the top and the most specific on bottom.

American women   American women astronauts   women
            human beings   Sally Ride

most general: _____
            _____
            _____
            _____
most specific: _____

Answer   Here is the best ordering.

most general: human beings
            women
            American women
            American women astronauts
most specific: Sally Ride

This example shows that the idea of general–specific is closely related to classification. The term human beings includes both women and men, so human beings is more general than women. Moreover, the term women includes American women as well as non-American women, so women is more general than American women. Going one step further, the term American women includes American women astronauts as well as American women nonastronauts, so American women is more general than American women astronauts. The term Sally Ride is most specific because it refers to just one person. Now try the following exercises.

Exercise 1. Write each of the following sets of terms in the spaces provided, with the most general on top and the most specific on bottom.

a. tomato soups   foods   liquid foods   Campbell's tomato soup
   soups

   most general: _____
                 _____
                 _____
                 _____
   most specific: _____

b. furniture   metal chairs   manufactured objects   chairs
   metal rocking chairs

   most general: _____
                 _____
                 _____
                 _____
   most specific: _____

c. Zenith color   communication   color   appliances
    televisions   appliances   televisions

    most general: _____
                  _____
                  _____
    most specific: _____

d. successful   successful   successful   successful   successful
    professional athletes   professional people   professional
    athletes   quarterbacks   football
                                                             players

    most general: _____
                  _____
                  _____
                  _____
    most specific: _____

Exercise 2: For each list, write something more general above the item already on the list, and something more specific below it.

List 1

more general: _____
                        meat
more specific: _____

Here is an answer for list 1.

more general: _food_____
                        meat
more specific: _beef_____

The term food includes meat as well as fruit, vegetables, and other edibles. So food is more general than meat. On the other hand, beef is one type of meat. So the term beef is more specific than meat. Use the same type of reasoning for the remaining exercises.

List 2

more general: _____
                        coat
more specific: _____

List 3

more general: _____
                        cars
more specific: _____

List 4

more general: _____
                  professional singers
more specific: _____

List 5

more general: _____
                        magazines
more specific: _____

List 6

more general: _____
                        doctors
more specific: _____

List 7

more general: _____
                  human-powered transportation vehicles
more specific: _____

Summary

This unit covered two patterns for arranging ideas: classification and general–specific. You may have noticed a relationship between the patterns. A classification has a topic and categories. The topic is general and each category is more specific. This relationship between the patterns is shown on the diagram.

Topic	↔	General
Category	↔	Specific
Example	↔	More Specific

Although the two patterns are related, they are used in different situations. When you are describing an entire set of things (like popular pets) you might classify them into categories and write a classification paper. But when you are writing a paper to prove the truth of a general statement, you try to think of two or three specific examples that support your statement, and then you present these examples with even more specific details. For example, in writing a paper entitled "Pets Are Useful To People," you would not write a classification paper on all pets. Instead, you would describe a few specific examples like German shepherds working as seeing eye dogs and monkeys being trained to aid cripples. Furthermore, to make your points clear and convincing, your paper would need specific details like how seeing-eye dogs help a blind person to avoid obstacles and to cross streets. You might even be more specific and describe a trip to the store by a blind man with his dog. Classification papers are illustrated in the next unit, whereas papers presenting general statements supported by specific details are covered in units 7, 8, and 9.

Unit

6

Classification

One way that people make sense of the world is to classify things into groups on the basis of similarities and differences. Potatoes, cabbages, spinach, and other such edible roots and leafy plants are classified together as vegetables, whereas sweeter, seed-bearing plants like cherries, apples, and pears are placed into a separate class called fruits. Another example is the Classified Telephone Directory (the "Yellow Pages"), where businesses are classified according to type: Accountants, Advertising Agencies, Automobile Dealers, etc. Because we think in terms of classifications, much of our writing reflects this organizational pattern.

Most classification papers deal with three to five categories of persons, things, actions, or ideas. Generally, two or three characteristics are focused on in describing the distinctive features of each category. For instance, one of the following exercises concerns the branches of the United States government. Each branch is described in terms of three characteristics: (a) type of activities; (b) parts or divisions; and (c) method for selecting officials. The entire paper has this outline.

Topic: Branches of the U.S. Government

    Category 1. Executive Branch
             a. type of activities
             b. parts or divisions
             c. officials

Category 2. Legislative Branch
      a. type of activities
      b. parts or divisions
      c. officials

Category 3. Judicial Branch
      a. type of activities
      b. parts or divisions
      c. officials

Some classification papers are a little more complicated and include subcategories within the main categories, as you will see in set 4 about varieties of cheese.

The wide range of topics lending themselves to the classification pattern is shown in the exercises that follow. Some classifications, like the branches of our government, were created systematically by men. Others, such as the varieties of cheese, evolved gradually over time and somewhat haphazardly. Finally, classifications like the "types of campers" in set 5 are caricatures, created as much to amuse as decribe. Working through the exercises will strengthen your ability to write informative English sentences tied together into a well-organized classification paper.

Writing For Learning

Many of the following exercises ask you to write sentences in the best logical order. To obtain the greatest benefit, do not copy the words letter-by-letter. Instead, use these steps for each sentence.

1. Read as many words as you believe you can write correctly from memory (usually five to 10 words).

2. Write those words from memory, including all capitals and punctuation marks.

3. Check back to the original sentence and correct any errors you made.

4. Read the next group of words and repeat the above steps.

Generally you will be able to read, memorize, and correctly write between five and 10 words. Sometimes you may be able to remember an entire simple sentence correctly. But with a large, difficult-to-spell word, you may only try to write that one word correctly from memory. Writing from memory will make you more aware of the spelling, grammar, punctuation, and word patterns used in standard written English.

SET 1. GRADES OF BEEF

A simple classification paragraph might briefly describe several categories for some group of things. The following sentences can be organized into a paragraph on the categories used for different grades of beef.

Exercise 1. Number the sentences to form a paragraph that begins with a question to arouse the reader's interest.

_____ It comes from young, well-fed animals and has lines of fat running throughout the meat, making it juicy and tender.

_____ The best quality beef is labeled Prime.

_____ When shopping for beef at the supermarket, have you ever wondered about the difference between cuts labeled Prime and those called Choice or Good?

_____ Choice is the second highest quality.

_____ But Good beef can be made tender and delicious by cooking it properly.

_____ Beef labeled Good has little fat and is less tender than the two better grades.

_____ Choice has less fat than Prime but is still juicy and tender.

_____ There are several grades of meat below these three.

_____ They are also used for ground beef and popular meat products like the all-American hot dog.

_____ Although not as tender, they can provide healthy, low-budget meals.

Exercise 2. Write the sentences in the order you numbered them to form a classification paragraph for grades of beef.

SET 2. MY CAR THE IMAGE

What's in a name? Do you buy products because of their names? The following sentences can be arranged into a brief classification paper taking a critical look at product name deception.

Exercise 1. Read the following sentences to get an overall impression of the main topic they deal with. Note that you have a choice on which pair of sentences to use for paragraph 1. Then do exercise 2.

Vocabulary
christen: name
mythical: not real, from a myth (type of story)
ploy: trick
Riviera: section of southern Europe with beautiful beaches and rich, glamorous people.
transport: move from one place to another.

Paragraph I

_____ Automobiles are a major part of modern American life, and most families own at least one.

_____ They vary in size, performance characteristics, price, image, and fuel economy—all to be considered when purchasing a car.

OR

Paragraph I

_____ Obviously the name of a car does not effect how it drives.

_____ However, manufacturers often give names to cars which suggest exciting or desirable characteristics that appeal to our emotions but cloud our thinking.

II

_____ Such names suggest the power and speed of wild, uninhibited beasts in nature.

_____ An old but still common trick is to christen automobiles with the names of real or mythical animals.

_____ Through the years we have seen Hudson's <u>Hornet</u>, Buick's <u>Wild Cat</u>, Mercury's <u>Cougar</u>, Ford's <u>Mustang</u> and <u>Thunderbird</u>, and Leyland's <u>Jaguar</u>.

III

_____ Buick's <u>Riviera</u>, Chrysler's <u>New Yorker</u>, and Pontiac's <u>Parisienne</u> fit into this category.

_____ Another ploy of car makers is to borrow names from pleasant or elegant places.

_____ Supposedly, stepping into these vehicles magically transports you from your dull hometown to the centers of the rich and glamorous.

IV

_____ Examples are Porsche's <u>911</u>, Chevrolet's <u>Z28</u>, Oldsmobile's <u>442</u>, and all the <u>GT</u> models.

_____ They also suggest associations with racing cars, which generally have large numbers or letters painted on them.

_____ These designations give the impression of high-tech mechanical perfection.

_____ The most recent trend has been to use numbers or letters as names.

V

_____ Pick a car for its performance and design qualities, not for what its name suggests.

_____ As an intelligent car buyer, guard against being fooled by such glamorous names and labels.

Exercise 2. Write the sentences into a paper about three categories of names that manufacturers use to sell cars. First decide which pair of sentences to use for paragraph 1. One paragraph is too broad for the rest of the paper. The other paragraph is tailor-made to introduce the topic under discussion.

Present the information in paragraphs 2, 3, and 4 in the same order: First write the sentence introducing the type of car name, then the sentence listing the sample of cars, and finally the sentence(s) analyzing the appeal of the category.

Exercise 3. With all material from the preceding exercises away, write a brief classification paper on automobile name deception. You may use any ideas or language that you remember from the paper, or you may draw upon your own experiences.

SET 3. CLASSIFICATION SYSTEM FOR U.S. GOVERNMENT

Can you write a description of the classification system underlying the activities of your own government? The following sentences can be arranged into a thumbnail sketch of the U.S. government.

Exercise 1. Number the sentences within each paragraph to form the best logical order. Describe each government branch (paragraphs 2, 3, 4) in terms of: (a) type of activities; (b) divisions or departments; and (c) officials.

Vocabulary
empowered: given power.
issues: controversies, topics under discussion
prevailing: dominating, occurring most frequently.
tyranny: government where one ruler has total power, often selfishly or cruelly.

I

_____ So they divided the activities of our government among three branches, preventing any single person or group from becoming too powerful.

_____ The writers of our constitution wanted to insure that the U.S. would be free from the tyranny of kings prevailing in Europe at the time.

_____ The three branches, created and empowered by the Constitution, are the Executive, Legislative, and Judicial.

II

_____ To perform these duties the Executive branch includes the Defense Department, with the Army, Navy, Air Force, and Marines; the Treasury Department, with the IRS, Customs Service, and Bureau of Engraving and Printing; the Justice Department (FBI); the Transportation Department; and many other agencies.

_____ The President is the chief of this branch, hiring or firing the department heads, and he (or she) is selected every 4 years in an election open to all citizens.

_____ The Executive branch executes (carries out) the country's laws and protects it during war.

III

_____ Each state elects two senators who represent it for 6-year terms, but the number of representatives (with 2-year terms) it sends to the House depends on its population: more population, more representation.

_____ This branch consists of the Senate and the House of Representatives, together called the Congress.

_____ Both the Senate and the House have many committees, such as the Finance Committee and the Foreign Relations Committee, which study issues and make recommendations on new laws, taxes, and national spending.

_____ The Legislative branch makes laws for the country and holds the "power of the purse" – the authority to levy taxes and decide how the money is spent.

IV

_____ Such judgments are needed when two people (or groups) differ in their interpretation of the law, or when the law has been broken and a judgment must be made about the appropriate punishment.

_____ The Judicial branch interprets and makes judgments about the law.

_____ Federal judges are appointed by the President and must be approved by the Senate.

_____ The appointments are for life, which helps free judges from political pressure.

_____ The work of this branch is done by district courts, appeals courts, and the Supreme Court.

_____ Most cases start in district courts.

_____ If he is still dissatisfied, he may try to take his case to the Supreme Court.

_____ If a person disagrees with the judgment of a district court, he can go to an appeals court and have the case judged again.

_____ The Supreme Court, which only handles cases of great national importance, has the final authority in legal judgments, and also the power to decide whether any new law violates the Constitution and must be changed or abolished.

V

_____ The proof is that for over 200 years the three branches have kept each other from assuming excessive power, while working together for the benefit of the nation.

_____ Dividing the activities of our government among three branches has functioned as the writers of our Constitution hoped it would.

Exercise 2. Write the sentences in the order you numbered them to form a classification paper on the U.S. government.

SET. 4. A CHEESE FOR ALL TASTES

Exercise 1. Number the following sentences to form a paragraph that:

1. first arouses a reader's appetite and interest in cheese;

2. then provides a little background information;

3. finally introduces a classification of cheeses.

I

_____ Over the years so many varieties have been developed that a person is almost sure to find one type appealing to the tastebuds.

_____ In fact, cheese is one of man's oldest foods, mentioned even in the Old Testament of the Bible.

_____ Pizza, cheeseburgers, cheese fondue, and cheese danish are just some of the delectable foods we would miss without cheese.

_____ The assorted cheeses you can buy in supermarkets and cheese stores fall into two categories, natural cheese and processed cheese; furthermore, natural cheese may be either unripened or ripened.

Exercise 2. Number the sentences in each paragraph to form a paper that continues the cheese classification just introduced.

II

_____ The whey is partially drained and the curd is refined into unripened cheese.

_____ The simplest cheese, unripened natural cheese, is made by adding rennet (derived from calf stomach enzyme) to milk.

_____ Rennet causes the solid material of milk to form into white lumps called curd, leaving just a thin liquid known as whey.

_____ Cottage cheese, made from skim milk, is an important food for dieters because it is rich in protein and other nutrients but low in calories.

_____ Three common unripened cheeses are Cottage, Ricotta, and Cream.

_____ Ricotta cheese, made from whole milk, is smoother than Cottage cheese and is used in tasty Italian dishes like lasagna.

_____ It is used in sandwiches and in baking the popular dessert, cheesecake.

_____ Cream cheese is the richest of the three because it is made from cream.

III

_____ By contrast, ripened cheeses are more flavorful because they go through an additional step in production.

_____ The unripened cheeses described above have mild flavors, as you probably know from tasting them.

_____ This is called ripening, and different cultures are used to give various cheeses their distinctive flavors and textures.

_____ Cultures (small living organisms) are added to the cheese and allowed to grow.

_5_ Ripened cheeses are labeled <u>mild</u>, <u>medium</u>, or <u>sharp</u> indicating the length of time they were ripened.

_____ Limburger, for example, is so soft it can be spread on crackers, Swiss is firm and usually sliced, while Parmesan is so hard it must be grated and sprinkled on food.

_____ Ripened cheeses also vary in softness, determined mainly by moisture content.

_____ The sharpest cheeses are produced through long ripening and may be labeled <u>aged</u>.

_____ In addition, Blue cheese and Roquefort are veined with blue streaks produced by the cultures used for ripening.

_____ Regarding color, ripened cheeses range from the flat white of Brick to the golden yellow of aged Cheddar.

IV

____ Emulsifiers make cheese blend smoothly, slice easily, and melt readily.

____ Other processed cheeses acquire their flavor from different natural cheeses and added ingredients like bacon or hickory smoke.

____ Besides the variety of natural cheeses just described, cheese merchants have provided customers with even more choices by creating processed cheese.

____ One popular processed cheese is American cheese, which has the natural cheese called Cheddar as its main ingredient.

____ Processed cheese is manufactured by grinding and mixing natural cheeses with emulsifiers and the aid of heat.

V

____ A variation of processed cheese has been given the name processed cheese food.

____ The milk also produces a milder flavor, which some people prefer to the strong flavor of natural cheese.

____ Processed cheese food is mixed like processed cheese, but milk or whey is added to make it softer and easier to spread.

____ The appeal of cold pack is not its ease in spreading but the delicious flavors created by blending fine, aged cheeses.

____ Another variation of processed cheese called cold pack is made by mixing well-aged natural cheeses without adding much emulsifiers or moisture.

VI

____ This provides an easy way to discover new, tasty cheeses that you can add to your menu in appetizers, sandwiches, and sauces, making one of life's basic pleasures, eating, even more pleasurable.

____ Most cities have cheese stores that offer bite-size free samples of numerous cheeses to help customers in their selection.

Exercise 3. Write the sentences in the order you numbered them to form a classification paper on cheese.

Exercise 4. In the last unit you arranged ideas into a classification pattern. The cheese paper basically has that pattern, although one of the categories (processed cheese) doesn't have subcategories but rather one example and two variations. Fill the blanks in the following outline for the cheese paper. Note: For Examples list specific cheeses like Cheddar, not qualities like "soft."

Topic: _____

  Category: _____

   Subcategory: _____

    Example: _____

    Example: _____

    Example: _____

   Subcategory: _____

    Example: _____

    Example: _____

    Example: _____

    Example: _____

    Example: _____

    Example: _____

  Category: _____

    Example: _____

   Variation: _____

   Variation: _____

SET 5. NOT ALL CAMPERS CAMP

The following sentences can be arranged into a light-hearted classification paper on campers.

Exercise 1. Number the sentences so they are logically ordered within each paragraph. If several arrangements are possible for a paragraph, pick the one you like best.

> Vocabulary
> habitation: residence, place where one lives.
> virgin: never used

I

_____ This quest for travel-adventure-on-a-budget has greatly swelled the population of campers.

_____ Americans have taken to the roads in a big way lately.

_____ And by spending a few nights at a campground, local or distant, one discovers there are three major types who seek such temporary habitation: those who sleep away from their vehicles (campers); those who "plan" to sleep away from their vehicles (pseudo-campers); and those who sleep in their vehicles (RV'ers).

_____ They are seeking new horizons, exploring historical spots once only read about, visiting the latest tourist attractions, yet trying to avoid sky-rocketing airline fares and motel rates.

II

_____ Their equipment is often expensive, but it is designed for years of use by people who prefer to face the elements of nature wherever they can—even if only at a KOA campground.

_____ When compared to motel motorists, jet-setting hotelers, or even RV'ers, the campers are not just bargain hunters but true lovers of camping.

_____ These modern day Daniel Boones are independent and self-sufficient.

_____ They enjoy chopping wood, cooking over an open fire, and ignoring the available electricity.

_____ These hearty souls realize the existing dangers (hungry animals, poisonous snakes, accidents), but brave it all just to really camp.

_____ Some in this group are so ardent that they avoid the camp-grounds of the masses and look for places in the actual wilderness to pitch their tents.

III

_____ For weeks, their neighbors listen to their plans to camp during the upcoming vacation.

_____ Next are the pseudo-campers.

_____ The car is loaded with the tent and other camping gear in anticipation of the adventure to come.

_____ A necessary part for putting up the tent has been forgotten; the weather is too hot (or too cold or too damp); or they find a motel room almost as cheap as the campground (and because they are really only camping to save money, it would be silly not to stay at the motel, even if the pool is tiny and overcrowded).

_____ However, there usually is something to prevent them from actually camping.

_____ Virgin or just sampled, the tent ends up in the trunk of the car until it can become the basement mildew farm.

_____ Sometimes these people do use their tents for a night or two, but they invariably decide that they simply do not enjoy camping.

IV

_____ Although it does cost a few extra dollars for the availability of electricity to use today's most modern conveniences, the RV'ers do not complain.

_____ They are not really bargain hunters.

_____ Finally, there are the RV'ers, who sleep in their vehicles on the other side of the campground from the true campers, in the "full hook-up" section.

_____ After all, some recreational vehicles cost as much or more than a small house—so what's a few more dollars.

_____ The high vehicle price and the estimated "dollar-a-mile" to make it run may explain why so many RV'ers seldom spend time away from their vehicles on vacations.

_____ Forget about nature; they're camping.

_____ An early evening tour of their section of the campground proves that most of them are "home": the air conditioners are running full blast, and the TV's are blaring their favorite programs while the steaks simmer in the microwaves.

V

_____ However, regardless of which type one is, camping offers the chance to trade everyday activities for new experiences away from home.

_____ Personal preference for conveniences, money, and the amount of daring one possesses usually are the deciding factors determining the type of camper one chooses to be.

Exercise 2. Write the sentences in the order you numbered them to form a classification paper on campers.

Analysis Of Classification Papers

The exercises in this unit illustrated classification paragraphs and papers. In starting your own classification papers, avoid the common error of choosing a topic that is too broad for the amount of writing you plan to do. For example, the car image paper gave you a choice between two opening paragraphs.

Choice 1   Automobiles are a major part of modern American life. They vary in size, performance characteristics, price, fuel economy, and image—all to be considered when purchasing one.

Choice 2   Obviously the name of a car does not effect how it drives. But manufacturers often give names to cars which suggest exciting or desirable characteristics that appeal to our emotions and so cloud our thinking.

The first choice introduces a topic that is too broad for the short paper that follows. In 250 words it is not possible to classify and describe automobiles in terms of size, performance, price, economy, and image. Such a paper would require at least 1,000 words to even briefly cover the necessary facts and examples. Always choose a topic that you can cover with sufficient detail in the length of paper you plan to write. Then formulate your opening sentences so they reflect exactly what the rest of the paper discusses. If your opening sentences promise more than your paper delivers, your readers will be unimpressed with you as either a writer or a solid thinker.

In addition to introducing the topic of a paper, a good opening may try to arouse a reader's interest. One common technique for snagging the reader's attention is to ask a question, such as: When shopping for beef at the supermarket, have you ever wondered about the difference between cuts labeled <u>Prime</u> and those called <u>Choice</u> or <u>Good</u>? If you ask the right question, a person will read further to find the answer.

Another technique is to excite the senses with a vivid, concrete description like: Pizza, cheeseburgers, cheese fondue, and cheese danish are just some of the delectable foods we would miss without cheese.

The last function that the introduction may serve is to provide a little background information on the topic, such as:

Americans have taken to the roads in a big way lately. They are seeking new horizons, exploring historical spots once only read about, visiting the latest tourist attractions, yet trying to avoid sky-rocketing airline fares and motel rates. This quest for travel-adventure-on-a-budget has greatly swelled the population of campers.

After the introduction, you begin to describe the categories. One way is with openings like these:

One type of . . . The first kind of . . . The cheapest category of . . .

The second group of . . . The next type is . . . Another kind of . . . Turning to the next category. . . .

The last category is . . . The final type is. . . .

Another method for introducing a new category is through comparison with a previous category, such as: Beef labeled <u>Good</u> is less tender <u>than the two better grades</u>.

But such beginnings are not always necessary. Often, just starting a new paragraph signifies a new category, and you can simply name and begin describing it with a sentence like: The Legislative branch of the government was empowered by the constitution to make new laws for the country.

In describing the distinctive features for each category, try to present the details in parallel (the same order) whenever possible. In the car images paper, each paragraph could be arranged to begin with the general statement about the type of car name, then present several examples, and finally explain the appeal of the category. If you changed this order for different paragraphs, the paper would appear confused and disorganized.

In some cases, a completely parallel description of all the details in each category may not be appropriate. You may emphasize different details in different categories because they have more significance. In the cheese paper, distinctive flavors were emphasized in describing ripened cheeses, but practicality for spreading and cooking was highlighted for processed cheese. Ripened cheese is valued for flavor, processed cheese for practicality. Generally, however, you will have the same two or three characteristics in mind as you describe all the categories. When your subject lends itself to parallel description of these characteristics, certainly use it for the clarity it adds to communication.

In bringing a short classification paper to an end, a separate concluding sentence or paragraph is not always necessary. You may just close with the last details of your final category, especially if you can end on a positive note that gives your readers a sense of closure. The meat grades paper ended with the positive qualities of the final category: Although not as tender, they can provide healthy, low-budget meals. They also are used for ground beef and meat products like the all-American hot dog.

But whenever possible, try to write a conclusion that draws your paper together. This is how the cheese paper was summed up.

Most cities have cheese stores that offer bite-size free samples of numerous cheeses to help customers in their selection. This provides an easy way to discover new, tasty cheeses that you can add to your menu in appetizers, sandwiches, and sauces, making one of life's basic pleasures, eating, even more pleasurable.

This conclusion has a positive tone because the entire paper was positive about cheese. Of course, for a paper taking a critical or negative view of the categories, the conclusion would summarize that position, as in the car images paper.

As an intelligent car buyer, guard against being fooled by such glamorous names and labels. Pick a car for its performance and design qualities, not for what its name suggests.

Both of these endings illustrate that an effective way to close a classification paper is with a general observation about the whole array of things you categorized. One more example is seen in the campers paper, which ended: . . . regardless of which type one is, camping offers the chance to trade everyday activities for new experiences away from home.

Independent Writing

In doing the following assignments, remember that good writers generally read through and revise a paper TWO or THREE times before considering it finished. After you write a first draft, read it from the beginning and revise sentences which can be expressed more clearly or smoothly. Also add any new ideas and examples that you think are important. REWRITE THE WHOLE PAPER IF NECESSARY. Finally, read your paper once more to catch spelling and grammar errors. This is the only way to write well.

1. Food may be categorized as meat (including seafood), dairy, grains (bread, noodles, cereal), and produce (vegetables, fruits). Write a classification paper (about 500 words) on these four categories of food. If there are important subcategories within the four broad categories, include them in the paper.

   Describe each category systematically. For each category you might first give examples of that type of food, then explain how the food is obtained, and finally describe how it is eaten.

   You will probably find it useful to first make an outline, grouping foods into categories and listing ideas you will write about for each category.

   If you have trouble thinking of ideas, try brainstorming for 3 minutes. You could write down every idea about food that comes into your mind. Or you could begin with meat, writing down every idea about meat that comes to mind: kinds of meat, how you cook them, etc. Then brainstorm for each of the other categories. After brainstorming, organize the ideas into a category-by-category outline. At the same time, try and think of sentences to introduce and explain the ideas for each category. Talk to yourself as if you were describing foods to someone else. Write down any useful sentences or paragraphs, because this will make your job of writing the paper easier. Then write a first draft of the paper, read it critically, and revise it to correct spelling or grammar errors, and to express and illustrate your ideas more clearly.

2. Write a classification paper on vehicles that travel the streets. For each category, present a physical description of the vehicle, its major use, and other relevant information.

3. Write a classification paper on TV shows. For each category in your paper, describe examples of specific shows and also the appeal or effect on the audience for that type of show.

   You might begin by brainstorming. Take one full minute to list all the shows and types of shows that you can think of. It might help to think of shows broadcast in the morning, in the afternoon, at dinner time, on Monday night, etc.

4. Think of three types of people, such as three types of drivers, students, athletes, dressers, or dancers. Then make up names for the three types. For dressers these might be "glamour boy," "slob," and "straight." Next, brainstorm for ideas to describe their appearance, actions, or other distinguishing characteristics. Include plenty of details so your readers can actually see the three types. Organize the ideas into an outline, including any sentences that you think of to introduce and express your ideas. Finally, write a classification paper on the three types, as was illustrated in the campers paper.

Unit

7

Generalization Supported by Specific Details

A generalization is a broad statement like "San Diego is a great place to live," or "My childhood prepared me well for adult life." To convince people that a generalization is correct, you must give them specific details that support or illustrate it. What makes San Diego a great place to live? The climate? The geography? The business or recreational opportunities? Specific details make your writing persuasive, interesting, and easier to understand.

Remember from unit 4 that the terms general and specific are relative, as shown in the diagram.

more general ┬ Increases in the cost of living
├ Increases in medical costs
more specific ┴ Increase in the cost of a hospital room

A paper might begin with this generalization: There has been a sharp increase in the cost of living over the past 10 years. Then each paragraph could describe a specific increase, such as the increase in medical, housing, or transportation costs. Within the paragraph on medical costs the writer could present illustrations that are even more specific, such as increases in hospital room and baby delivery bills. The overall paper would have this form.

Paragraph 1.	Generalization Introduced	There has been a sharp increase in the cost of living over the past 10 years, as seen by the rise in medical, housing, and transportation costs. Etc.
Paragraph 2.	Support I	Medical expenses have increased. Examples: hospital room and baby delivery fees.
Paragraph 3.	Support II	Housing costs have increased. Examples: buying, renting and heating costs.
Paragraph 4.	Support III	Transportation costs have increased. Examples: purchase, repair and fuel prices.
Paragraph 5.	Conclusion	Generalization restated and ideas summarized.

The following exercises begin with illustrations of how individual paragraphs are made interesting and convincing by including specific details to support generalizations. The exercises then progress to three- and four-paragraph selections and eventually an eight-paragraph paper, all with the generalization–specifics pattern. The topics range from personal concerns, such as choosing a pet, to public issues like false advertising or the location of a city's convention center.

Writing For Learning

Many of the following exercises ask you to write sentences in the best logical order. To obtain the greatest benefit, do not copy the words letter-by-letter. Instead, use these steps for each sentence.

1. Read as many words as you believe you can write correctly from memory (usually five to 10 words).

2. Write those words from memory, including all capitals and punctuation marks.

3. Check back to the original sentence and correct any errors you made.

4. Read the next group of words and repeat the above steps.

Generally you will be able to read, memorize, and correctly write between five and 10 words. Sometimes you may be able to remember an entire simple sentence correctly. But with a large, difficult-to-spell word, you may only try to write that one word correctly from memory. Writing from memory will make you more aware of the spelling, grammar, punctuation, and word patterns used in standard written English.

SET 1. YOU CAN'T AFFORD TO BE SICK

A generalization is a broad statement. Here is an example of a generalization.

Generalization: Hospital costs have skyrocketed since the 1970's.

When you state a generalization, you usually need one or more examples to make the generalization clear and convincing, as illustrated in this exercise.

Exercise 1. Number the following sentences to form a paragraph that begins with a generalization and then supports it with examples. One sentence has already been given the number 4.

> Vocabulary
> bear: give birth to (also: carry, stand up under)
> unbearable: too painful or difficult to stand
> delivery: delivery of a baby

_____ For example, in 1975 a bed in a semi-private room at Boston Memorial was $95 a day.

_____ Now the bill for the same room is $200 a day.

_____ Hospital costs have skyrocketed since the 1970's.

__4__ It has even become unbearably expensive to bear children.

_____ But last week 7 lb. Billy Wilson cost his parents $900 to be born there: about $130 a pound.

_____ Manhattan General Hospital charged $400 for a normal delivery in 1975 (not counting the physician's fee).

_____ Again this did not include the physician's fee, which also more than doubled during the period.

Exercise 2. Write the sentences in the order you numbered them to form a paragraph supporting the generalization that hospital costs have skyrocketed.

SET 2. PICK GOOD SUPPORTING EVIDENCE

In writing a convincing generalization-specifics paper, it is important to include specifics that really support your generalization. Ideas that are only loosely associated with the generalization may sometimes be worked into the paper to arouse interest and to provide background information. But the weight of your argument must be carried by direct supporting evidence.

Exercise 1. Only four of the following eight sentences support the statement: Trees provide us with many benefits. Write those four sentences in the space provided. You may write the four sentences in any order.

We must be careful to prevent forest fires because it takes years for trees to grow back in a burned area.

Apples, pears, and many other fruits come from trees.

The largest and oldest living things in the world are the California Redwoods, some of which stand over 300 feet tall and have been growing since the days of the ancient Greeks.

Huge quantities of lumber from trees are used by the home construction and furniture industries.

If we don't plant new trees to replace the ones we cut down, our children won't have any.

When the pilgrims came to America, there were trees stretching from the east coast to the west coast, except for some plains and desert areas.

The shade of a tree can be a great comfort on a hot summer day.

Trees absorb carbon dioxide and give out oxygen, which humans need to breathe.

Trees provide us with many benefits.
1.
2.
3.
4.

Exercise 2. From the remaining sentences, write two that could be used in discussing the history of trees.
1.
2.

Exercise 3. Write the two sentences dealing most directly with the conservation (saving and protection) of trees.

1.

2.

SET 3. THE WONDERFUL PLASTIC CARD

Exercise 1. The following sentences include a general statement about credit cards and supporting illustrations. Number the sentences within each paragraph to form the best logical order.

Vocabulary
ceases: ends
domestic: related to the home or one's home life.
financial: related to money.
in short: in summary, to summarize, all in all.
moreover: furthermore, in addition.
stability: lack of change, reliability, permanence.

I

_____ You can go to a department store and pick out a giant-screen TV, fine stereo, or warm winter coat, then enjoy it while paying on time.

_____ At home it increases your buying power for larger, more expensive items.

_____ A credit card is an extremely useful little piece of plastic, both at home and on a trip.

II

_____ Cash or travelers cheques won't satisfy them.

_____ On a trip the card permits you to purchase meals, lodging, gas, and souvenirs without carrying a wallet stuffed full of $20 and $50 bills.

_____ But the piece of plastic identifies you as a responsible person with some domestic and financial stability, a person whom they'll trust with one of their vehicles.

_____ In fact, if you try to rent a car during your trip, you'll find you won't be able to get one from any of the major auto rental agencies without a credit card.

III

_____ Moreover, as soon as you report the card stolen to a 24-hour telephone number, your financial responsibility ceases.

_____ Generally, there is a $50 limit on your responsibility for someone else's illegal use of your card.

_____ In short, a credit card gives you all the purchasing power of continually carrying several hundred dollars, but none of the risk.

_____ Perhaps most important, whether you are at home or traveling, you don't have to worry about your credit card getting lost or stolen, the way loose cash can cause worry.

Exercise 2. Write the preceding sentences in the order you numberthem.

Exercise 3 (optional). With all of the preceding materials out of sight, write a short paper arguing that credit cards are (or are not) very useful.

SET 4. THE COMPANY NEEDS A NEW TRUCK

When you recommend an expensive purchase like buying a new truck, you need convincing reasons with specific facts to win your case. The following sentences can be arranged to make a well-supported argument for a new truck.

Exercise 1. Number the sentences within each paragraph to form the best logical order.

I

_____ Nevertheless, we should buy a new truck because the old truck is unreliable, obtaining parts for it is difficult, and the greater economy of a new truck would help repay the purchase price.

_____ It is true that new trucks are expensive and the company's budget is tight.

II

_____ Worst yet, last Friday it quit running on the expressway and had to be towed to a garage.

_____ Three times last month deliveries to customers were late because the truck would not start.

_____ The company is sure to lose business if this continues.

_____ The old truck is constantly breaking down.

III

_____ This means they have to special-order the parts, which usually takes several hours and once took 2 days.

_____ Another problem is getting replacement parts.

_____ Because of its age, most repair shops don't carry the hoses, belts, mufflers, or other parts it requires.

IV

_____ Our old clunker only gets about 12 miles per gallon on the highway and less in the city.

_____ There are not only the savings on repair costs, but we can choose a truck that gets much better gas mileage.

_____ Looking at the brighter side, a new truck would eventually pay for itself.

_____ All things considered, buying a new truck makes a lot of sense.

_____ Some of the newer models average as much as 30 or 40 miles per gallon.

Exercise 2. Write the sentences in the order you numbered them to form a short paper that expresses an opinion that a certain action should be taken, then supports that opinion with three specific reasons (including examples).

SET 5. THE PERFECT PET

What is the perfect pet? The following sentences present one opinion along with supporting details.

Exercise 1. Number the sentences within each paragraph to form the best logical order.

Vocabulary
astronomical: very large
crustacean: shellfish like a crab or lobster
domicile: home, place where one lives.
feisty: quarrelsome, full of nervous energy
habitat: home or home territory
partiality: preference, liking for something

I

____ When you add that it is odorless, quiet, and a super traveling companion, you will begin to understand my partiality for this creature.

____ This feisty little crustacean is inexpensive to buy and keep, and it does not have to be housebroken.

____ If you are thinking about acquiring a new pet, let me suggest that you consider a hermit crab.

II

____ Most pets cost much more, and their purchase price is just the beginning of an expensive relationship.

____ Being in the right pet store at the right time (because hermit crabs are sometimes difficult to find) is all you must do to get one of these pets for less than $5.

__3__ The average pet, especially a furry one, requires regular veterinarian visits for shots to prevent rabies and distemper, treatment of various illnesses and accidents, and medicines to fight heart worms, stomach worms, ticks, and fleas.

_____ Fish owners must first buy an elaborate tank system and then spend more money maintaining the delicate balances of temperature and water chemistry that are required within this domicile.

_____ Finny friends stay out of the doctor's office, but their housing costs are high and can easily become astronomical.

III

_____ With a little imagination you can make its habitat from leftovers and inexpensive materials.

_____ A hermit crab, on the other hand, neither sees a doctor nor demands a costly, elaborate home.

_____ Add a few twigs for climbing, a shallow dish for water, and some kitty litter, cedar shavings, or shredded newspaper for a hiding place, and this pet is practically "home free."

_____ A recycled leaky fish tank will make an excellent cage.

IV

_____ Just the elimination of this housekeeping routine makes it an ideal pet as far as I'm concerned.

_____ Because a hermit crab is such a light eater, its body wastes are so minimal that its cage only needs to be cleaned every 2 months.

_____ You never have to rush home from work to take it out for a walk so it can eliminate its wastes in front of someone else's house instead of in yours.

_____ You also completely avoid the tasks of teaching it to use a newspaper and cleaning up when it doesn't.

V

_____ Other pets can cause large odor problems.

_____ Another charming attribute of a hermit crab is that it is odor free.

_3_ Most pet owners who have a dog, cat, or other four-legged or winged animal have discovered that the amount of effort needed to avoid unpleasant and lingering pet odors grows in direct proportion to the animal's size.

_5_ You may not notice the change in the air around you, but others will.

_____ And if your house is indeed your pet's house, no amount of care can assure that a foul smell won't spread throughout your home as the pet roams about while you are away.

VI

_____ But a hermit crab is always a silent partner.

_1_ Other people may also be annoyed by the various sounds pets make.

_____ To me there is nothing more irritating than a dog that barks at anything that moves or a cat that howls at other cats as they prepare to fight or romance each other.

VII

_____ Of course, you could leave yours at home because it can easily survive for 2 weeks without care (providing it has enough water and food in its cage).

_____ Because hermit crabs are so quiet, they also make super traveling companions.

_3_ However, should you elect to take your hermit along, no special travel arrangements will be needed.

_____ "No Pets" signs may be ignored with total confidence.

_____ Your pocket or palm makes a perfect traveling compartment wherever you roam.

__6__ No one will ever know you are traveling with your pet unless you volunteer a peek.

_____ And one doggie bag could keep it well fed for years.

_____ Even dining on the road is not a problem because your hermit crab can get by the most scrutinizing hostess or maitre d'.

VIII

_____ Those nifty creatures sell very quickly because the public is beginning to realize what a unique and undemanding friend a hermit can be.

_____ If you would like to know more about hermit crabs as pets, the best way is to try sharing your life with one.

_____ I suggest that you call a pet store and request that one or two hermits be saved for you when the next shipment arrives.

Exercise 2. Write the sentences in the order you numbered them to form a paper arguing that hermit crabs are great pets.

Exercise 3. (optional) Write a paper (minimum 150 words) about which animal you would like most for a pet and why. If the animal is a hermit crab, make sure all materials from exercises 1 and 2 are away. If you would not want to own any pet, write a paper explaining your reasons.

SET 6. ORDERING SUPPORTING DETAILS

When you present several specific examples to support a statement, you may order them from least to most impressive so that your argument ends on a strong point. This is illustrated in the first exercise.

Exercise 1. Following are three examples supporting the statement: Medical science has made wonderful progress in its fight against disease since 1900. Rank the examples from least impressive (oldest) to most impressive (newest) by writing the numbers 1, 2, and 3 in the spaces provided. (Vaccines were developed before transplants.)

> Vocabulary
> genetic engineering: creating new forms of life
> ultimate: most important, final
> vaccine: type of medicine taken to prevent a disease

_____ Parts of the body, such as the heart and kidney, have been transplanted from one person to another.

_____ Work on the ultimate medical problem, the creation of life itself, has advanced as far as test-tube babies and genetic engineering.

_____ Vaccines have been developed against measles, yellow fever, and polio.

Exercise 2. The three sentences you just ranked have been reproduced along with seven others below. Number the sentences to form a paragraph with the following arrangement.

1. Begin with a generalization about progress in our century compared to earlier times.

2. Present one supporting statement followed by several examples and then another supporting statement with its examples.

3. Close with a sentence that reinforces the opening generalization by comparing the 20th century favorably with later time periods.

Vocabulary
century: 100 years
innovative: producing new things, original, creative
spectacular: terrific, striking, sensational
20th century: the 100 years from 1900 to 2000

_____ For example, medical science has made wonderful progress in its fight against disease since 1900.

_____ Considering it took humans thousands of years to learn to make simple tools like knives and plows out of iron, the scientific and technical advances of our own century are spectacular.

_____ Also, parts of the body, such as the heart and kidney, have been transplanted from one person to another.

_____ Even work on the ultimate medical problem, the creation of life itself, has advanced as far as test-tube babies and genetic engineering.

_____ Vaccines have been developed against measles, yellow fever, and polio.

_____ Astounding progress has been made outside of medicine as well.

_____ Most recently, nuclear energy has been harnessed to provide electrical power for homes and industry, and computers have been developed that solve problems faster than the human brain.

_____ One can hardly imagine any future century being more innovative than ours, the 20th century.

_____ Airplanes have been invented, jet engines have made air travel faster, and rockets have carried men to the moon.

_____ The short span of the 20th century has given us Xerox machines, televisions, and automobiles.

Exercise 3. Write the sentences in the order you numbered them to form a long paragraph on progress in our century.

SET 7. BUYER BEWARE

Do you believe the promises made in magazine advertisements? The following sentences can be organized into a paper claiming that much advertising is false.

Exercise 1. Number the sentences within each paragraph to form the best logical order.

Vocabulary
fleecing: stealing through trickery.

I

_____ Millions of teenagers as well as adults believe these ads and send in their dollars for the promise of a lovelier figure or a fuller head of hair.

_____ Magazines are filled with advertisements promising spectacular improvements in your appearance quickly and with little effort.

_____ But unfortunately the only people who benefit from most of the advertised miracle products are the fast-buck salesmen who collect the cash.

II

_____ As soon as you drink any liquid, the weight returns to exactly the body area where it was originally.

_2_ The ads say they will take 2 inches off your waist or hips in just hours.

_____ Rubber waist bands and plastic shorts, sometimes called "spot reducers," are prime examples of such money-making gimmicks.

_____ In short, the spot reducers are not just worthless; they can be hazardous.

_4_ But medical studies show that weight loss from sweating is not permanent.

(more sentences on next page)

_____ They work by causing excessive sweating in the part of the body covered.

_____ What is worse, the tight rubber (or plastic) clothing can interfere with normal circulation, leading to blood clots, and can make the body overheat to a dangerous degree.

III

_2_ The Food and Drug Administration warns that most ingredients sold for weight control without a prescription have not been shown to be safe or effective.

_____ The FDA concluded that diet pills should not be used for more than 3 months, and that a permanent weight loss will only occur if a person changes his or her eating habits.

_____ In fact, out of 111 ingredients contained in over-the-counter weight control drugs, the FDA found that only 2 were effective.

_____ One ingredient, benzocaine, dulls the nerve endings in the mouth.

_____ Another group of widely advertised, quick cure products are diet pills.

_____ The other, phenylpropanolamin hydrochloride, curbs the appetite but also raises blood pressure, which is potentially dangerous.

IV

_____ Unfortunately, no proven remedy for baldness has yet been found.

_____ With the possible exception of Kojak, baldness is generally not considered attractive, so middle-aged men are easy victims for the hair grower ads.

_____ Some products claim they rub protein into your hair, but this is as senseless as rubbing pork chops on your biceps to build your arm muscles.

_____ But when you shower or go swimming, the coating disappears.

_____ A third popular product for fleecing unsuspecting consumers is hair growing tonic.

_____ At best, the products put a coating on your hair to make it appear thicker.

V

_____ The safest way to protect yourself against false advertising is to remember that whenever a product seems "too good to be true," it probably is just that.

Exercise 2. Write the sentences in the order you numbered them to form a paper cautioning consumers.

SET 8. MISPLACED CONVENTION CENTER

Do you always agree with government decisions? When you disagree, can you write a clear explanation of your reasons in order to convince others of your opinion? The following sentences can be arranged to explain several reasons why the writer disagrees with a city council decision.

Vocabulary

convention: a large gathering of people in the same business or having a common interest, like a 3-day meeting of lawyers from around the country.

convention   large building used for conventions, concerts, or
center: other big meetings and entertainment events.

enhanced: made larger or better.

foresight: concern and good planning for the future.

inherent: built-in, natural.

loathe: hate.

merge: join together.

monstrosity: large, abnormal thing, freak.

patron: customer.

premium: best, special, expensive.

site: location, place where something is or occurred.

Exercise 1. Number the sentences within each paragraph to form the best logical order.

I

_____ Now it is almost completed, and I loathe it.

_____ The primary reasons for my attitude are that the chosen site wastes the beach's inherent beauty and ability to draw tourists; it wastes an opportunity for economic growth in the western, inland section of town; and it strains the beach's natural and man-made environments almost to the point of destruction.

_____ Last year the officials of my city, Daytona Beach (a resort on the east coast of Florida), voted to build a new convention center right across from the ocean.

II

_____ People will pay top dollar to temporarily or permanently live by the sea.

_____ Wherever there is a beach, you are sure to find competition to use all of the available space.

_3_ The space taken by the convention center could have been used to build an attractive beach-side hotel or apartment complex that would have drawn additional tourists to the town and fully utilized the economic potential of beach property.

_____ Had the city officials used greater foresight in planning, the area could have become a showcase for the entire East Coast with a free-spending tourist population to match.

_____ Moreover, viewing the ocean at sunrise, or under a full moon, or during a violent storm—these wonderful experiences were lost for countless people when a convention center was built instead of living rooms and bedrooms overlooking the Atlantic.

III

_____ A westward location would have permitted the center's patrons to be closer to the array of attractions already in that area.

_____ Next, the chosen site wastes an opportunity for the economic development of the inland area west of the beach.

_3_ These attractions (dog track, jai alai games, auto racing, two shopping malls, and several restaurants) are tailor-made for the partying and shopping needs of conventioneers.

_____ In this and other ways, a western site would have raised the value of a large parcel of land that does not have the natural premium value of beach property.

_____ All of these businesses would have benefited from the increased patronage by conventioneers, and additional businesses could have been built because there is plenty of room for expansion on the inland side of town.

IV

_____ When an audience packs in for a concert by a famous performer, the smells created by the trash and sewerage will mask those of the fresh salt air; the noises from heavy traffic will drown out the sounds of the waves; and the view of the seashore will be less enjoyable with 15,000 extra people milling about.

_____ Finally, the most devastating problem is the strain that the chosen site will put on the natural and man-made resources of this area.

_____ The natural resource is the beach, with its view, its smells, its sounds, and its shoreline.

V

_____ The next bridge has four lanes, but it too was built at least 40 years ago.

_____ Because the site, like most Florida east coast beaches, is located on a long, narrow island separated from the mainland by a river, it can only be reached by bridge.

_____ A major strain will also be placed on the man-made resources.

_____ The road and bridge closest to the new center are only two lanes wide and very old.

__5__ It will be a traffic nightmare when crowds merge at these bridges to get across the river to attend an event at the convention center.

_____ However, the collapse of one of the bridges should be a concern for everyone who plans to use them either to attend a major event or to travel to and from the beach during the weeks that follow.

_____ I hope it is only minor fender benders and impatience that these people will have to face.

VI

_____ But the beach is unique with pleasures that cannot be duplicated or enhanced except by keeping the surrounding areas clean and well maintained.

_____ All in all, I wish the beach area had been left alone to be enjoyed as "the Beach."

_____ It is a shame that those in power did not realize this before it was too late.

_____ The monstrosity of concrete and glass could have gone elsewhere and been patronized just as well.

Analysis Of Generalization–Specifics Papers

This unit illustrated paragraphs and papers organized in the generalization–specifics pattern. As shown in exercises 4 through 8, a persuasive 250–600 word paper of this type usually includes at least three pieces of specific supporting evidence. And each of these is backed up with even more specific examples. Specific details expand on a generalization, capturing the reader's imagination and clarifying the writer's meaning.

Starting a Generalization–Specifics Paper. Exercise set 3 (Credit Cards) involved a short paper (around 250 words) that did not have a separate introductory paragraph. The generalization was stated, and then the first supporting detail was immediately described in the opening paragraph. Set 7 (False Advertising) had a longer paper of around 450 words. The entire opening paragraph was devoted to introducing the generalization and to providing a little background information. Set 8 (Convention Center) had an opening paragraph that not only introduced the generalization but that also previewed the three specific points used to support it. This is an effective way to begin a generalization–specifics paper; it is discussed extensively in the next unit.

Defending an Opinion. Sometimes a generalization is an opinion that others might disagree with. A good way to begin such a paper is to mention the opposing arguments in the introduction, but then to show how your position deals with them. An example of this was seen in exercise set 4; the paper began, "It is true that new trucks are expensive and the company's budget is tight." In this way the writer acknowledged the financial problems of buying a new truck and then addressed them in the paper.

The Hermit Crab paper took a somewhat different approach. Because the thesis was that a hermit crab is the best of all possible pets, the paper contrasted hermits with other common pets to show their virtues regarding cost and convenience. In this way the writer tried to anticipate some of the arguments from lovers of other pets.

Ending a Generalization–Specifics Paper. An important caution should be noted on how not to end a generalization–specifics paper. Do not introduce a new idea in the conclusion. Inexperienced writers sometimes cannot think of how to end a paper, so they start off on a new point. For example, in the Convention Center paper they might try to create a thought-provoking ending by saying that the city council was guilty of several other bad decisions over the last few years. Or in the Credit Card paper, an inexperienced writer might think it would make the ending more interesting to say that travelers cheques also are useful. But such endings are unconvincing because there is no opportunity to support the new ideas with examples and specific details.

It is better to end a paper of this type by simply summarizing your generalization and perhaps tieing it together with some of your specific support. For a short paper, this usually can be done with one sentence. The Credit Card paper ended, "In short, a credit card gives you all the purchasing power of continually carrying several hundred dollars, but none of the risk." When you can avoid a phrase like "in short" or "in summary," it is better to do so because these phrases are used very often in papers. But if you cannot think of a way to avoid such a phrase, go ahead and use one because it will give you a solid footing for closing the paper. The False Advertising paper illustrates a closing sentence that does not use a phrase like "in summary," but still does summarize the main idea of the paper: "The safest way to protect yourself against false advertising is to remember that whenever a product seems 'too good to be true,' it probably is just that."

The Hermit Crab and Convention Center papers were longer—over 450 words—so they used separate paragraphs for conclusions. The Convention Center paper summarized the main ideas in a final paragraph this way.

All in all, I wish the beach area had been left alone to be enjoyed as "the Beach." The monstrosity of concrete and glass could have gone elsewhere and been patronized just as well. But the beach is unique with pleasures that cannot be duplicated or enhanced except by keeping the surrounding areas clean and well maintained. It is a shame that those in power did not realize this before it was too late.

Notice that this paragraph does not introduce any new ideas. Instead, it strongly restates the author's opinion and summarizes some of the supporting arguments.

In the present chapter you arranged sentences into generalization-specifics papers. Because this is such an important writing pattern, the next two chapters are devoted to helping you write your own original papers of this type.

Unit

8

Beginning With a Thesis Statement That Includes an Opinion and Supporting Evidence

This unit teaches a technique for writing a paper that convincingly defends an opinion. The ability to write such a paper is useful when you are trying to sway people to take some action. It also is useful in writing papers to pass writing competency tests—an immediate concern to many students.

The technique consists of starting with a thesis statement that presents an opinion and also lists the evidence supporting it. The remainder of the paper explains the supporting evidence with specific details. This unit takes you through the steps of applying the technique in writing your own paper.

Section 1 Two Parts Of The Thesis Statement

The first step is to write the thesis statement. Your thesis statement is a summary of your entire paper. It states an opinion or point of view, and also previews the evidence you will use to support that opinion. Here is an example of a thesis statement.

> Thesis Statement: Daytona Beach is a great place to take a vacation because of its warm climate, good beaches, reasonably priced motels, and major auto/cycle race track.

Notice that this thesis statement has two parts: (a) a statement of opinion; and (b) a list of the supporting evidence. Here are the two parts.

a. Statement of opinion: Daytona Beach is a great place to take a vacation.
b. Supporting evidence: warm climate, good beaches, reasonably-priced motels, major race track.

Now try these exercises.

Exercise 1. Write the two parts of the following thesis statement in the spaces.

> Thesis Statement: Swimming is one of the best forms of exercise since it tones the muscles, decreases the risk of heart attack, and does not strain the back or joints.

a. Statement of opinion: _____
b. Supporting evidence: _____

Exercise 2. Write the two parts of the following thesis statement in the spaces provided.

> Thesis Statement: New York City is a wonderful place to live because it has good public transportation, a wide range of job opportunities, many schools and colleges, and hundreds of movies, theaters, restaurants, night clubs, and other forms of entertainment.

a. Statement of opinion: _____
b. Supporting evidence: _____

Section 2 Writing Your Thesis Statement

If you are like most people, you have many opinions. You believe some things are good or worthwhile, whereas others are bad or useless. Perhaps you think a certain baseball star is the best player that ever lived, that a certain car would suit your needs perfectly, or that some city would be nice to visit. Maybe you dislike some teacher, school subject, or occupation. Perhaps you feel cigarettes should be taxed $20 a pack. Use one of your opinions for the next exercise.

Exercise 1. Pick one of your opinions that you can support with at least two pieces of evidence. Write the opinion and supporting evidence in the form of a thesis statement.

Thesis Statement: _____

_____

_____

Section 3 Presenting Specific Details For The Supporting Evidence

The second step is to write one or more paragraphs giving details to explain each piece of supporting evidence in your thesis statement. Here is how this could be done for the thesis statement about Daytona Beach.

Daytona Beach is a great place to take a vacation because of its warm climate, good beaches, reasonably priced motels, absence of traffic problems, and major car/cycle race track.

The climate in Daytona is warm; snow is virtually unknown. While the northern states are slick with ice in January and February, the daytime temperature in Daytona averages around 70 degrees, permitting people to sunbathe and go boating or fishing. By March, the temperature climbs to 80 degrees, and the ocean is warm enough for swimming. Even in the evening the temperature is mild enough that all you need is a sweater to go out and have dinner or fun at the discos.

Daytona has a 15-mile strip of beach that is free to the public. Furthermore, you can drive onto the beach, park your car, and put your blanket or beach chair beside it. Thus you avoid paying high parking fees, or searching for an hour to find a parking space and then walking many blocks to reach the ocean.

To complete this paper you would write a paragraph on the reasonable prices of motels and another paragraph on the excitement of the car and cycle races. Finally, you would write a conclusion paragraph that summarizes your main points.

If your thesis statement only listed two pieces of supporting evidence, then you should present more details for each one in order to defend your opinion. For example, in the preceding paper you might spend several paragraphs describing the pleasures of the warm climate and the fun on the beach.

Now it is your turn; try the exercise.

Exercise 1. On a sheet of paper, copy the thesis statement you wrote earlier. Then, for each piece of evidence in your thesis statement, write at least one paragraph explaining it with examples and details. Finally, write a conclusion paragraph that summarizes your main points. (If you encounter difficulty writing a conclusion paragraph, review page 125).

Section 4 Taking Writing Competency Tests

The technique you just learned can be especially useful for passing writing competency tests. On such tests you generally are given a list of general topics. You are asked to pick one topic and write a paper on it. Try these steps.

1. Pick a topic on which you have a viewpoint or opinion that you can support with several examples or pieces of evidence.

2. Write a thesis statement of the type presented in this chapter.

3. Make sure to present enough details and examples to fully explain and illustrate each of your supporting points.

4. Write a conclusion paragraph that summarizes your main points.

If you follow these steps and use standard, grammatically correct English, your paper will be seen as well organized and well written. The next unit provides additional guidance in writing a paper of this type.

Remember, however, that you are not required to use the opinion-support pattern on many competency tests. For some tests your paper might describe a person or a place, as illustrated by papers in unit 2. Or your paper might describe a series of exciting or humorous actions, like the Raw Rage and The Practical Unjoker papers of unit 4. In some cases you might combine several of the patterns identified in this book. If you are asked to write a paper on any modern appliance (TV, telephone, microwave), you could begin with a physical description (unit 2), then explain its functions and provide instructions for its use (unit 4), and finish with several examples showing its vital role in our lives (unit 7). Use any combination of patterns that allows you to best express your ideas.

Unit

9

Writing a Paper for a Competency Test: Brainstorming for Ideas

The last unit presented a procedure for writing a paper expressing and supporting an opinion on some topic. The procedure can be used in writing to newspaper editors, congressmen, employers, or anyone else whom you are trying to convince of some viewpoint. The procedure also can be used for writing papers on exams such as those required for admission to or graduation from many educational institutions, as well as employee selection tests given by major companies. This unit expands on that procedure by showing you a technique you can use to get a paper started on a writing test. The technique helps you think of material that you can develop into a well-organized paper.

Section 1 What Decisions Do People Make?

Tests of writing skill often give you two or three very broad topics and ask you to write a paper of around 500 words (in about an hour) on one of the topics. Of course you may write a well-organized paper using any of the patterns covered in other chapters: cause–effect, comparison–contrast, classification, and so forth. But one of the easiest ways to write an effective paper in the limited time and without other sources of information is to use the opinion-support (also called generalization–specifics) pattern discussed in the last two units.

One way to help identify opinions or general statements you can express on a topic is to ask yourself, "What decisions do people make regarding the topic?" For example, suppose one of the broad topics is Buying A Car. What decisions do people face and what questions do they have on the topic of buying a car?

Should I buy a new or used car?
Should I buy a car or a motorcycle?
Should I buy a car or use public transportation?
Which car should I buy?
What factors should I consider in buying a new car?
Can I afford a new car? What is the price range?
What size car should I buy?

Now place yourself in the position of answering the questions and making the decisions. How would you decide and why? Would you buy a new or used car? What factors do you consider important in buying a car? Why did you buy your car (if you have one)?

Your answers to these questions—your opinions—are candidates for a 500-word paper. But before going on to the next step, try these exercises.

Exercise 1. Write as many decisions and questions which you can think of that a person might face on the topic Going To College.

Broad Topic: Going To College

Question 1: _____
Question 2: _____
Question 3: _____
     Etc.

Exercise 2. Write as many decisions and questions which you can think of that a person might face on the topic Playing A High School Or College Sport.

Broad Topic: Playing A High School Or College Sport

Question 1: _____
Question 2: _____
Question 3: _____
        Etc.

Exercise 3. Write as many decisions and questions which you can think of that a person might face on the topic Careers.

Broad Topic: Careers

Question 1: _____
Question 2: _____
Question 3: _____
        Etc.

Exercise 4. Write as many decisions and questions which you can think of that a person might face on the topic Living In (Your City or State).

Broad Topic: Living In (Your City or State)

Question 1: _____
Question 2: _____
Question 3: _____
        Etc.

Section 2 Brainstorming For Information And Opinions

Do you have any opinions or information regarding the questions you wrote in the last section? If you immediately think of an opinion or answer to one of the questions, which you can support with several examples, you may be ready to begin writing a paper.

But if you do not immediately think of anything useful, try brainstorming about the questions you wrote. Brainstorming means letting as many ideas as possible come into your mind and writing them down quickly without judging or trying to organize them. Here are the questions that were written earlier on buying a car. Next to them is a list of ideas that came to mind while brainstorming about these questions. Notice that the ideas from brainstorming are not written in sentences. They are just written as quickly as they come to mind.

Decisions & Questions	Ideas From Brainstorming
Should I buy a new or used car?	new cars cost more, used cars need repairs, leaking radiator, breakdown on road, rebuild transmission, expensive
Should I buy a car or motorcycle?	motorcycles are dangerous, motorcycles are cheap and fun
Should I buy a car or use public transportation?	buses, trains, taxis, sometimes must wait a long time for a bus or train and they may not be easy to reach
Which car should I buy?	buying a new car—cost, handling, appearance, mileage, size, power, comfort
What factors should I consider in buying a car?	big cars good for large families and carrying things, big cars pollute the the air more and use more gas—leads to shortage
Can I afford a new car? Which size car should I buy?	Seville—$26,000, Chevette—$6,000. My Cougar—good ride, handles well, sleek design

The brainstorming list may now contain enough ideas for a paper. The next step is to try and use some of them in writing a thesis statement. But first do the following brainstorming exercises.

Exercise 1. In the last section you wrote questions about decisions related to the topic Going To College. Some sample questions are presented. Read the questions. Then brainstorm for ideas related to these questions and the questions you wrote earlier.

General Topic: Going To College

Sample Questions   Brainstorming Ideas
_____   _____

Should I go to college? Why?
What should I major in at college?
What factors should I consider
   in selecting a major?
Which college should I attend?
What factors are important
   in picking a college?
How will I pay for college?

Exercise 2. Here are some sample questions about decisions related to the topic Playing A School Sport. Brainstorm for ideas related to these questions and the questions you wrote earlier.

General Topic: Playing A School Sport

Sample Questions   Brainstorming Ideas
_____   _____

Should I play a school sport?
What are the benefits of playing
   a school sport?
What are the disadvantages of
   playing a school sport?
What sport should I play?
Are women given an equal chance?

Exercise 3. Here are some sample questions about decisions related to the topic Careers. Brainstorm for ideas and answers to these questions and the questions you wrote earlier.

General Topic: Careers

Sample Questions   Brainstorming Ideas
_____   _____

Which career should I choose?
Which careers will offer me the
   income I desire?
Which career would I enjoy?
For which careers do I have the
   education or preparation to
   start work immediately?
Which careers require more than
   just a H.S. diploma?

Exercise 4. Here are some sample questions about decisions related to the topic Living In Your City Or State. Brainstorm for ideas related to these questions and the questions you wrote earlier.

General Topic: Living In Yourtown

Sample Questions   Brainstorming Ideas

Is Yourtown a desirable place to live?
What are the employment opportunities
   in Yourtown?
What are the entertainment and
   social attractions of Yourtown?
How expensive is housing in Yourtown?
What is the climate in Yourtown?

Section 3 Writing A Thesis Statement

After brainstorming for ideas on a topic, you are ready to try and write a thesis statement. One of the easiest thesis statements to write and support with examples is the statement that certain factors should be considered in making a particular decision. Here is an example for the topic Buying Cars.

Three important considerations in buying a new car are price, size, and annual costs.

This basic idea can be developed into an interesting paper not only for a writing competency exam but even, if done well, for a magazine like *Consumer's Reports* or *Reader's Digest*. If you add a few introductory sentences to arouse a reader's interest, and then follow your thesis statement with useful information on purchasing a car, people will not only enjoy your paper but will even pay for the privilege of reading it in a magazine. Here is a sample introduction; perhaps you could write a better one.

As a member of modern society, you probably often need to travel distances greater than you can walk. You may travel several miles to work, to school, to shopping centers, to the doctor, and to other places. The result is that a large portion of your income is spent for transportation, and THESIS STATEMENT ──────▶ for many Americans this means a car. When purchasing an automobile, three important considerations are price, size, and annual cost.

Automobiles vary greatly in price. For the money you pay to buy one of General Motor's luxury cars like the Cadillac Seville, you can own four of the company's subcompacts. Or you can own one subcompact, a boat, a camper, and a 40″ TV. Therefore. . . .

Notice in the preceding example how the background information leads up to the thesis statement, which in turn leads to the first supporting paragraph.

The thesis statement in the above example merely presented factors that should be considered in making a decision. It did not express an opinion about an important decision. A second type of thesis statement does express an opinion about a decision, which it supports with evidence. Here are two examples based on the brainstorming list.

A Mercury Cougar is a good car to buy because it has a comfortable ride, it handles well, and it is not too expensive.

Unless you frequently need a large car to transport people or goods, you should buy a small car because it saves you money, helps conserve oil, and pollutes the air less.

Now try the following exercises in which you will write thesis statements based on your own brainstorming.

Exercise 1. Using your brainstorming list from the last section, write the following two types of thesis statements about going to college.

Thesis Statement 1. Write a thesis statement on factors that should be considered in some decision about going to college.

Thesis Statement 2. Write a thesis statement expressing an opinion supported by two or more pieces of evidence regarding a decision about going to college.

Exercise 2. Same as exercise 1 for the topic Playing A School Sport.

Exercise 3. Same as exercise 1 for the topic Careers.

Exercise 4. Same as exercise 1 for the topic Living In Your City Or State.

Section 4 Writing A Thesis Paragraph To Express A Mixed Opinion

If you want to express a mixed opinion – both the good and bad sides of an issue – you may require more than one sentence to do the job of the thesis statement, namely, state the opinion and also preview the supporting evidence. Here is an example of a mixed opinion and its supporting evidence expressed in a four-sentence paragraph.

Living in Manhattan has both good and bad points. On the positive side, there are endless employment, cultural and entertainment opportunities. But you never get away from the noise of people and machines, and there is no chance to enjoy nature. In fact, because of the traffic congestion and parking problems, you can't even enjoy the pleasure of driving your own car to work, to stores, or to go out with friends.

Write similar paragraphs for the next exercises.

Exercise 1. Write the following sentences so they first express a mixed attitude on a topic and then preview the supporting details.

_____ The initial cost of a used car is lower, and it will generally depreciate less than a new car does over the first 3 years.

_____ Finally, a new car may add to a person's professional image or personal pride.

_____ There are disadvantages and advantages to buying a new car.

_____ But there is the expense and inconvenience of more repairs with a used car than a new one.

_____ Furthermore, a new car has the latest equipment for improved handling, mileage, and acceleration.

Exercise 2. Following is a list of attractions and drawbacks of living in Daytona Beach. Write a short paragraph expressing a mixed opinion about living in Daytona and previewing the supporting evidence.

Attractions

mild year-round climate; good beaches, golf course, tennis courts and other outdoor recreational facilities; major auto/cycle track; relaxed tourist-town atmosphere.

Drawbacks

limited industry and employment opportunities; weak on cultural facilities like museums, theaters, libraries, and fine restaurants; no snow
or ice sports; snow really missed at Xmas; tourists cause severe traffic
jams during racing season.

Exercise 3. Write a short paragraph expressing a mixed opinion and
previewing the supporting evidence on one of these topics.

Going To College; Playing A School Sport; Careers; Living In Your
City Or State.

Section 5 Writing And Checking The Final Paper

Once you have written the thesis statement or paragraph, writing the
complete paper simply involves adding several paragraphs with your
supporting details, along with an introductory paragraph to arouse
interest and a conclusion paragraph to summarize your main ideas.
For each of your supporting paragraphs, include specific examples
(with names, prices, or other information) to make your ideas clear
and convincing.

Before you actually begin to write the paper, it is usually profitable
to spend about 10 minutes making a rough paragraph-by-paragraph
outline. For each paragraph, write down the examples and details that
you will use to support your ideas. If any good sentences expressing
your ideas come to mind, write these down for later use. Preparing an
outline (even a rough one) will make the job of writing your paper
much easier.

One final note. As you write the paper, plan to save about 5 minutes
to reread and check. You will usually find some spelling and grammar
errors. You may even see a better way to express an idea. Your paper
will make a stronger impression if you take the time to polish off its
rough edges.

Section 6 Planning Your Exam Time

Here is the way you might allot your time for a 50-minute writing
exam. Make appropriate adjustments if you are allowed only 30 minutes or a whole hour.

1. (5 minutes). Decide whether you can make a statement or express an opinion about one of the topics, which you can illustrate or

support with three paragraphs of information and details. If you can, go straight to step 3. But if no such ideas come immediately to mind, pick one topic and start writing down decisions and questions people face regarding it. If other ideas or information about the topic come to mind, write them down also.

2. (3 minutes). Brainstorm for answers and information to the questions from stage 1. Write down all ideas that come to mind. They might be useful later.

3. (3 minutes). Write a thesis statement that expresses your position and previews the supporting material.

4. (9 minutes). Make a rough, paragraph-by-paragraph outline. Think of concrete examples that can be used for each paragraph. Also, think about how you would introduce or express ideas. If any good sentences come to mind, write them down. Include all of this in your outline.

5. (25 minutes). Write the paper using your outline. Include a short introductory paragraph to arouse interest and a conclusion paragraph to summarize your position.

6. (5 minutes). Read the entire paper carefully for spelling and grammar errors. Also look for awkward phrasing that could be improved.

Now try the exercise.

Exercise 1. Treat this exercise like a writing competency exam with a 50-minute time limit.

Write a paper of about 500 words on one of the following topics.

Going To College; Nuclear Energy; Playing A School Sport; Schools And Drugs; Careers; Living In Your City or State.

OTHER COMPETENCY-TEST PAPERS   If the opinion-support pattern does not fit the topics on a competency test, use another pattern or a mixture of patterns. For example, suppose one of the topics is: *Describe and discuss an invention of the past 100 years.* If you decide to write about the automobile, you might begin with a physical description of an automobile (unit 2), then include some material on its history or operation (unit 4), and finally present examples to show its importance (unit 7). Or, if a topic lends itself to a description of a place or a person, you might present a physical description interwoven with human actions and reactions, as illustrated in the Cafeteria and Steel Drums papers of unit 2. Use any combination of patterns that fits the topic (See page 175).

Unit

10

Comparing and Contrasting

When you compare two things, you describe their similarities. When you contrast them, you describe their differences. A comparison/contrast paper generally compares and contrasts two things on a number of points, showing how they are alike in some ways and different in others. One way to begin a comparison/contrast paper is with a chart like this for James Bond (agent 007) and Superman.

James Bond (007) vs. Superman

	James Bond	Superman
similarities	1. fictitious superhero ⟷	fictitious superhero
	2. attractive male ⟷	attractive male
	3. fights crime ⟷	fights crime
	4. always wins ⟷	always wins
differences	5. fights crime for pay —∦—	fights crime for justice and mankind
	6. no disguises —∦—	two identities
	7. enjoys the company of —∦— women	secretly and shyly loves Lois Lane
	8. uses technology —∦— extensively: modern weapons, sport cars, helicopters, tricky devices	depends on own power: superhuman strength, ability to fly, x-ray vision, bulletproof body

When you make a chart like this, the ideas generally will not come into your mind all neatly arranged with the similarities first and then the differences. Instead, the ideas may come somewhat haphazardly. But write down all the ideas as they enter your mind so you won't forget them. Later you can arrange them according to similarities and differences, as well as their importance and human interest value.

Once you have a chart, you are almost ready to begin a comparison/contrast paper. But you still have a decision. Should you write all about one superhero first and then all about the other one, as pictured below?

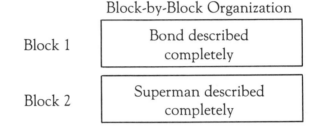

Or should you describe Bond and Superman on point 1, then Bond and Superman on point 2, and so on, covering the points of similarity in the early paragraphs and the differences in the later ones?

Point-by-Point Organization

Bond similar to Superman on point 1.
Bond similar to Superman on point 2.
Bond similar to Superman on point 3.
Bond similar to Superman on point 4.

Bond different from Superman on point 5.
Bond different from Superman on point 6.
Bond different from Superman on point 7.
Bond different from Superman on point 8.

The first type of paper is called a Block-by-Block pattern, whereas the second is a Point-by-Point.

In deciding on a topic for a comparison/contrast paper, pick things that are somewhat similar. It is easier to compare a Chevy with a Cadillac than an airplane with an apple. In a real-life business situation, your boss is more likely to ask for a comparison/contrast report on two models of typewriters rather than a comparison/contrast between a typewriter and a duplicating machine.

As you work through the exercises of this chapter, remember you are sharpening a skill that many people use to earn good incomes by writing comparison/contrast reports of products for magazines, handbooks, and manuals published by most large companies.

Writing For Learning

Many of the following exercises ask you to write sentences in the best logical order. To obtain the greatest benefit, do not copy the words letter-by-letter. Instead, use these steps for each sentence.

1. Read as many words as you believe you can write correctly from memory (usually five to 10 words).

2. Write those words from memory, including all capitals and punctuation marks.

3. Check back to the original sentence and correct any errors you made.

4. Read the next group of words and repeat the above steps.

Generally you will be able to read, memorize, and correctly write between five and 10 words. Sometimes you may be able to remember an entire simple sentence correctly. But with a large, difficult-to-spell word, you may only try to write that one word correctly from memory. Writing from memory will make you more aware of the spelling, grammar, punctuation, and word patterns used in standard written English.

SET 1.

When you compare two things, you describe their similarities. When you contrast them, you focus on their differences. This is illustrated in the following sentences.

Exercise 1. Five of the following sentences make comparisons, pointing out similarities between two things. The other four are contrasts, highlighting differences. Decide whether each sentence forms a comparison or contrast, and then write it in the appropriate space.

Vocabulary
exhausted: used up.

---

1. A microphone and a human ear are both sensitive to the small movements of the air produced when any sound is made.

2. The ball used in ping pong is smaller and lighter than the one used in tennis.

3. The N.Y. *Times* and the N.Y. *Post* are two high-circulation newspapers.

4. A sedan has four doors, whereas a coupe only has two doors.

5. Brick cheese is solid white, but blue cheese has bluish-green veins.

6. The world supply of oil and the supply of coal will eventually be exhausted.

7. Spanish is the official language in many South American countries as well as Spain.

8. A door and a bottle cap share the purpose of keeping things in or out.

9. Pedro had a better opportunity to get an education than his older brother.

Comparison Sentences (highlighting similarities)

1.
2.
3.
4.
5.

Contrast Sentences (highlighting differences)

1.
2.
3.
4.

SET 2. COMPARISON/CONTRAST PARAGRAPH

The following sentences can be arranged into a paragraph that compares and contrasts two popular fruits.

Exercise 1. Number the sentences in the best logical order, with the first three comparing plums to peaches and the remaining three contrasting them. One sentence has already been numbered 2.

_____ Moreover, plums are generally one color—red or purple— whereas peaches are multicolored: red, yellow, and a light shade of orange named "peach."

_____ Both fruits are juicy and sweet when properly ripened.

_____ Finally, each has a distinctive flavor, although this cannot be fully described but must be tasted.

__2__ They are larger than berries so people generally eat just one or two at a time, but they are smaller than melons so they are not divided and shared.

_____ Plums and peaches are both round, medium-sized fruits.

_____ But plums have a smooth skin, whereas peaches are fuzzy.

Exercise 2. Write the sentences in the order you numbered them.

Exercise 3. With the book closed and all material from exercises 1 and 2 out of sight, write a comparison/contrast paragraph on any two fruits.

SET 3. POINT-BY-POINT CONTRAST PAPER

A paper does not have to both compare and contrast two things. It can just compare them, or it can just contrast them. The following exercises illustrate a paper that just contrasts dogs with cats. The paper is organized to contrast dogs with cats on one point or characteristic, then on a second point, and finally on a third point. Therefore it is called a Point-by-Point contrast.

Exercise 1. Here are three characteristics on which dogs can be contrasted with cats.

	Dog	Cat
Personal Needs	Needs to be walked.	Uses litter box.
Noise	Barks, which makes it a good burglar alarm but sometimes too noisy.	Quiet.
Companionship	Close companion to humans.	More independent of humans.

The following sentences are about the three characteristics in the table.

1. Write an I in front of the sentence that could be used as an Introduction for a short paper contrasting dogs with cats.

2. Write an S in front of the sentence that could be used as a Summary for the paper.

3. Write PN in front of the three sentences dealing with the Personal Needs of dogs and cats.

4. Write N in front of the three sentences concerning Noise.

5. Write C in front of the five sentences concerning Companionship (not the Summary sentence).

> Vocabulary
> city dweller: person who lives in the city.
> not an unmixed blessing: having both good and bad effects, advantages and disadvantages.

_____ All in all, dogs take a little more trouble but repay your efforts with greater companionship.

_____ A cat can be trained to use a litter box in the house.

_____ Second, a dog can serve as a burglar alarm, barking when anyone approaches your door.

_____ If you are a city dweller who has decided to get a pet, and you have narrowed it down to either a dog or a cat, here are some factors to consider in making the final choice.

_____ This is not an unmixed blessing, however, because the litter box can be an unpleasant sight, can produce odors in the home, and does need to be cleaned.

_____ A cat is much quieter.

_____ First, a dog is a greater inconvenience because it must be walked twice a day, even when it is raining or cold outside.

_____ Finally, a dog tends to be a closer companion, following you around and always glad to be petted.

_____ And out of doors they are more likely to run off rather than follow you around.

_____ But some dogs carry this to an extreme, annoying you and your neighbors by barking at the slightest noise anywhere nearby, or for causes totally unimaginable to humans.

_____ But often they are happier to hide under the sofa rather than sit at your feet.

_____ Although there are exceptions, cats are usually less friendly.

_____ Occasionally they like to be petted or scratched.

Exercise 2. Write the sentences as a three-paragraph paper with the following form.

1. For the first paragraph, begin with the sentence you labeled I. Then write the sentences you labeled PN, describing the dog first and putting the sentences in the best logical order.

2. For the second paragraph, write the sentences you labeled N. Describe the dog first and put the sentences in the best logical order.

3. For the third paragraph, write the sentences you labeled C. Describe the dog first and put the sentences in the best logical order. End the paragraph with the sentence labeled S.

SET 4. BLOCK-BY-BLOCK CONTRAST PAPER

The paper you wrote in the last exercise contrasted dogs with cats on one point, then it contrasted them on a second point, and finally on a third point, producing a point-by-point organization.

Another way to contrast dogs with cats is to first write about dogs on all three characteristics and then write about cats, emphasizing how they differ from dogs on the three characteristics. This is called a Block-by-Block pattern.

The two patterns are shown in this diagram.

Point-by-Point Contrast

1. Contrast dogs with cats on one characteristic or point.

2. Contrast dogs with cats on a second point.

3. Contrast dogs with cats on a third point.

Block-by-Block Contrast

1. Describe dogs on all three characteristics.

2. Describe cats on all three characteristics, emphasizing contrasts with dogs.

Exercise 1. The following sentences can be used to write a paper contrasting dogs with cats on the same three characteristics as the last exercise, but using the Block-by-Block pattern.

1. Write an I in front of the sentence that could be used as an Introduction for such a paper.

2. Write S in front of the sentence that could be used to Summarize and end the paper.

3. Write D in front of the three sentences that are primarily concerned with Dogs. Be careful: One of the 12 sentences begins by describing dogs but ends with its main purpose—describing cats.

4. Write CP in front of the two sentences about the Cat's Personal needs.

5. Write CNC in front of the five remaining sentences. These CNC sentences are about a Cat's Noise and Companionship.

Vocabulary

antics: silly, clownish behavior

_____ Man's best friend, the dog, is a greater inconvenience because it must be walked twice a day, even when it is raining or cold outside.

_____ A cat, by contrast, does not need to be walked daily but can be trained to use a litter box in the house.

_____ If you are a city dweller who has decided to buy a pet, and you have narrowed it down to either a dog or a cat, here are some major considerations in making the final choice.

_____ But on the positive side, a dog can serve as a good burglar alarm, barking when anyone approaches your door.

_____ This is not an unmixed blessing, however, because the litter box can be an unpleasant sight, can produce odors in the house, and does need to be cleaned.

_____ A dog also tends to be a closer companion, following you around, always glad to be petted, and often barking or nudging you to play.

_____ As opposed to the silly antics and noisiness of many dogs, a cat is a nice quiet roommate.

_____ And it doesn't constantly pester you for attention.

_____ It doesn't bark every time anything passes anywhere near your home, driving you and your neighbors to distraction.

_____ All in all, a cat provides pleasant although cooler companionship than a dog, and it intrudes less on your time and other activities.

_____ Occasionally it greets you or comes over for pets and scratches.

_____ But generally it respects your right to privacy and is content to live with you in peaceful coexistence.

Exercise 2. Write the sentences in the form of a three-paragraph paper. For the first paragraph, begin with the sentence you labeled I, then write the sentences labeled D in the best logical order. For the second paragraph, write the sentences labeled CP in the best logical order. For the third paragraph, write the CNC sentences in the best logical order. Finish with the sentence labeled S.

SET 5. CHOCOLATE FREAKS TAKE NOTE

If you like chocolate, you are not alone. However, do you know about another product, carob, that tastes similar to chocolate but is much healthier? This is the subject of the following comparison/contrast paper.

Exercise 1. The sentences in the first paragraph describe similarities between chocolate and carob. The second and third paragraphs describe differences. Number the sentences within each paragraph to form the best logical order.

Vocabulary
nutrients: ingredients providing nourishment such as protein or vitamins.
pod: a part of certain plants that contains seeds (e.g., pea pod).

I

_____ But another tasty treat called carob is similar enough in flavor that it can be substituted for chocolate in most recipes.

_____ To make chocolate, the seeds are dried, roasted, and ground into a brown powder.

_____ For example, you can buy chocolate chip cookies or carob chip cookies, chocolate brownies or carob brownies, chocolate or carob ice cream, chocolate or carob shakes and hot drinks, and chocolate or carob candy bars.

_____ Most people like chocolate.

_____ For carob, the pods go through the same process, producing a brown flour.

_____ Both chocolate and carob come from trees with large pods containing seeds.

II

_____ Furthermore, chocolate is naturally bitter whereas carob is sweet.

_____ First, chocolate contains more natural fat than carob — about 52% fat in chocolate compared to only 2% in carob — making it higher in calories.

_____ Therefore a greater quantity of sugar is required to make chocolate tasty, and this contributes additional calories.

_____ Although carob and chocolate are similar in appearance and taste, carob is healthier for a number of reasons.

_____ Besides fewer calories, another advantage of carob is that it is rich in protein, vitamins A and B, and the minerals phosphorus and calcium.

_____ Instead it contains caffeine, a stimulant which, in large quantities, can make a person nervous or jittery.

_____ Chocolate also gives many people upset stomachs and allergic reactions.

_____ Chocolate, by contrast, has no such nutrients.

III

_____ In fact, about 2 billion pounds of chocolate are consumed in the United States annually, much more than the amount of carob eaten.

_____ Only time will show whether carob can overtake chocolate in popularity.

_____ Despite the health advantages of carob, at present most people choose chocolate products because they prefer its flavor.

Exercise 2. Write the sentences in the order you numbered them to form a short Point-by-Point comparison/contrast paper on chocolate and carob.

Exercise 3. The sentences in the first paragraph describe chocolate. The second paragraph describes carob, and the third describes the relative popularity of the two flavors. Number the sentences within each paragraph to form the best logical order.

I

_____ The seeds are dried, roasted, ground into a powder, and then made into consumer products.

_____ It is used in making brownies, chocolate ice cream, chocolate shakes and hot drinks, chocolate chip cookies, and, of course, chocolate candy bars.

_____ Most people like chocolate.

_3_ Chocolate comes from a tree with large seedpods.

_____ Unfortunately for dieters, chocolate contains about 52% fat, which makes it high in calories.

_7_ Other than fat, chocolate has no nutrients.

_____ Furthermore, because it is naturally bitter, large quantities of sugar must be used to make it tasty, and this contributes additional calories.

_____ Another drawback of chocolate is that it causes upset stomachs and allergic reactions with many people.

_____ Instead, it contains caffeine, a stimulant which, in large quantities, can make a person nervous or jittery.

II

_____ But for carob, the pods rather than the seeds are dried, roasted, and ground into a brown flour.

_____ For example, you can buy carob brownies, ice cream, shakes, hot drinks, carob chip cookies, and carob candy bars.

_____ Because of chocolate's disadvantages, many nutrition experts recommend another tasty treat called carob, which is similar enough in flavor that it can be substituted for chocolate in most recipes.

_____ Carob contains only 2% fat, making it lower in calories than chocolate.

_____ Like chocolate, carob comes from a seedpod-bearing tree.

_____ Another advantage of carob is that it is a nutritious food, rich in protein, vitamins A and B, and the minerals phosphorus and calcium.

_____ Finally, carob does not contain caffeine, nor does it cause upset stomachs or allergic reactions.

_____ Furthermore, it is naturally sweet, so little if any sugar needs to be added to make it tasty, saving even more calories.

III

_____ But it isn't.

_____ It seems chocolate has an evil grip on people's tastebuds, and carob doesn't have enough "flavor power" to break the spell.

_____ In fact, about 2 billion pounds of chocolate are eaten in the United States each year, many times the amount of carob consumed.

_____ With all of carob's health advantages, you might expect it to be consumed in larger quantities than chocolate.

Exercise 4. Write the sentences in the order you numbered them to form a short Block-by-Block comparison/contrast paper on chocolate and carob.

Exercise 5. Copy the following outline on a separate piece of paper or make your own outline based on exercises 2, 4, and your own experiences with chocolate and carob. Then put away other materials and write a comparison/contrast paper on chocolate and carob, using the outline and your own experiences. Remember that you generally must write a paper twice before it is well-organized, well-written, and fit for others to read.

Chocolate vs. Carob

<u>Similarities</u>. Similar taste. Both used in brownies, ice cream, cookies, etc. Both from trees with seedpods. For chocolate, seeds are dried, roasted, and ground into powder. For carob, pods dried, roasted, powdered.

<u>Differences</u>. Carob healthier: Lower in fat (2% vs. 52%); not bitter (so less sugar added); contains protein, vitamins A and B, minerals phosphorus and calcium; no caffeine (nervousness); doesn't cause upset stomachs or allergic reactions. Two billion pounds of chocolate eaten annually in U.S. Much less carob consumed.

SET 6. MCDONALD'S VERSUS ARBY'S

Most Americans frequently eat what is called "fast food." Which fast food restaurant is better, McDonald's or Arby's? Here is one person's opinion. See if you agree.

Exercise 1. The following sentences describe similarities between McDonald's and Arby's. Number the sentences to form the best logical order.

_____ Because the menus are limited, the food comes quickly.

_____ They offer a few additional food items, but basically they both have limited menus rather than the variety of foods available in regular restaurants.

_____ Finally, casual dress and children are welcome at both fast food chains.

_____ McDonald's and Arby's are fast food chains with locations throughout the country.

_____ Moreover, the limited menus combined with the absence of table service result in reasonable prices.

_____ Both chains offer the most popular fast foods: burgers, fries, and shakes.

Exercise 2. The following sentences describe differences between McDonald's and Arby's.

1. Write G by the <u>G</u>eneral statement contrasting McDonald's with Arby's on price, portion size, and tastiness.

2. Write H by the five sentences dealing with <u>H</u>amburgers (actually cheeseburgers).

3. Write F by the two sentences dealing with <u>F</u>ries.

4. Write Sh by the two sentences dealing with <u>Sh</u>akes.

5. Write O by the three sentences dealing with <u>O</u>ther items on the menu.

6. Write <u>Sum</u> by the Summary sentence.

> Vocabulary
> bland: dull, plain
> gustatory: related to the sense of taste.
> palatable: tasty, pleasing to the palate (part of the mouth).

_____ For example, McDonald's Big Mac, costing $1.67 and weighing 7 ounces, has cheese, special sauce, lettuce, pickles, onion and a sesame-seed bun.

_____ McDonald's fries, 62¢ for 3 ounces, are crispy and delicious.

_____ Moreover, the Big Mac's meat is tender and has a hearty beef flavor.

_____ McDonald's items tend to be a little more expensive than Arby's, but the portions are larger and the food is tastier.

_____ By contrast, Arby's cheeseburger, costing $1.45 for 5½ ounces, is plain and unappealing.

_____ Arby's fries (55¢ for 2½ ounces) are also crispy, but they are a little greasier and have a frozen potato taste somewhat like cardboard.

_____ The bun is bland, lacking crispiness or flavor.

_____ McDonald's chocolate shake (79¢) has a rich cocoa flavor.

_____ The meat has a strong, gamey flavor and a grisly texture, and the cheese tastes heavily processed rather than natural.

_____ In summary, the small additional cost of eating at McDonald's seems a worthwhile investment in gustatory pleasure.

_____ Turning to other items on the menu, McDonald's sells Chicken McNuggets (small pieces of batter-fried chicken) as well as fish sandwiches.

_____ Arby's special feature is a roast beef sandwich consisting of a plain bun, dry, gray meat, and no sauce or gravy.

_____ By contrast, Arby's chocolate shake (also 79¢) has a weak, artificial flavor and leaves a chalky coating in the mouth.

_____ The McNuggets and the sandwiches are highly palatable and have flavorful sauces.

Exercise 3. Write a two-paragraph comparison/contrast paper on McDonald's and Arby's. For the first paragraph, use the sentences you numbered in exercise 1. For the second paragraph, begin with the sentence you labeled G, next write the sentences you labeled H in the best logical order, then those labeled F, Sh, O and Sum.

Exercise 4. Write a comparison/contrast paper in the Block-by-Block format for any two fast food restaurants. Use information from the preceding paper or your own experiences. Note that conditions may have changed in the two restaurants just described. Also, you may have a totally different opinion than that expressed here.

SET 7. FILM OR PRINT

Which do you prefer, a good book or a fine movie? Here are some of the major similarities and differences between books and movies.

Exercise 1. Number the sentences within each paragraph to form the best logical order.

> Vocabulary
> cinematography: movie making.
> immersed: covered and surrounded by something—like a pot immersed in water for cleaning; giving something your total attention—like being immersed in a book.
> portable: movable, capable of being moved and used in different places.
> vicarious: experienced through someone else's activities—like a father getting vicarious pleasure when his son scores a touchdown.

I

_____ Others insist that when a movie is made from a fine book, the movie is never as good as the original.

_____ Reviewing the similarities and differences between books and movies can help a person be a better judge of this controversy which began almost as soon as movie making.

_____ Some people say that going to see a movie is better than curling up and reading a book.

II

_____ Within that message they both create vicarious experiences in which you can become totally immersed.

_____ Both begin with the basic purpose of transferring a lasting message to a distant audience.

_____ Books and movies share important similarities.

_____ You live the lives, experience the situations, and feel the emotions of the main characters, who may be spies, great artists, aging sports heroes, murderers, royalty, or common people dealing with everyday problems.

III

_____ They can take you back to the crowded streets of Rome, put you into the cockpit of a jet fighter plane, or move you forward 50 years when the earth is recovering from a nuclear war.

_____ Both books and movies provide you with avenues into the past, present, and future.

_____ They can make you look at society, at other people, and at yourself.

__5__ The ability to create these scenarios and arouse emotions is the greatest similarity between movies and books.

_____ Sometimes the view is pleasant and tender, as in peaceful or romantic scenes; sometimes it is not, as in stories of crime, war, and poverty.

IV

_____ The most basic difference is that participation in these two media demands the use of different mental processes.

_____ In spite of the similarities between books and movies, there are major differences between them.

_____ Reading a book depends on skills developed over a long period of training and experience.

__4__ Using and enjoying books requires the ability to read well enough to create mental images of the characters, visual settings and sounds.

__6__ The magic of cinematography produced stunning scenes like the Red Sea parting in *The Last Commandments* and Captain Ahab trapped in the ropes as the great white whale disappeared into the ocean in *Moby Dick*.

_____ Movies, on the other hand, provide ready-made pictures for your eyes and sounds for your ears.

_____ Movies bring all of this to people, even if they cannot read and create detailed mental images from print.

_____ The voices of Marlon Brando's whispery-gruff Godfather (*The Godfather*), Clark Gable's sensuous Rhett Butler (*Gone With The Wind*), and Judy Garland's melodious Dorothy (*The Wizard of Oz*) have been enjoyed by young and old alike.

V

_____ Nor did the Disney animated film *Bambi* express the plight of animals in the forest as intensely as did the German author in his original, bulky volume.

__2__ Books usually offer a more in-depth view of people's thoughts and feelings, whereas movies often limit themselves to outward actions.

_____ Another difference between these media is the depth in development of the story and characters.

__4__ The sheer horror felt by the victims in the book *Christine* was not conveyed in its film counterpart.

_____ For instance, the film version of *Gone With The Wind* omits the emotional pain shared by Scarlett and Rhett at the birth and death of their daughter.

VI

_____ However, to see a film you must often be in a certain place at a certain time.

__2__ Books are portable and can be used at your convenience, in the setting of your choice.

_____ The physical requirements of reading a book and viewing a movie are also very different.

_____ As a moviegoer, you must rely on your memory of the experience or be willing to wait and pay to see the film again.

__5__ Moreover, books give you the freedom to savor your favorite parts over and over again whenever and wherever you wish.

_____ You must be ready to experience the entire presentation in a theater where the environment may be unpleasant because of the noise, temperature, or smells.

VII

_____ Both have their own merits and offer experiences that can enrich our lives.

_____ Nevertheless, books are irreplaceable as my favorite media because I can enjoy them at my own convenience, and they usually provide a deeper understanding of people and situations.

_____ In summary, I cannot say that all books are better than all movies, or vice versa.

Exercise 2. Write the sentences in the order you numbered them to form a comparison/contrast paper for books versus movies.

Exercise 3. Make a table (like that for set 3) contrasting books and movies. You can use information from the preceding paper or from your own experiences. Then put all other material away and write a short paper contrasting books with movies. Conclude by stating which you prefer and why.

Analysis Of Comparison/Contrast Papers

Many essay exams and papers assigned in school require comparison and contrast. In a sociology class you might be asked to compare and contrast the political attitudes of American white collar workers with that of blue collar workers. In history you might be asked to contrast Spanish with English colonialization of the New World. In political science you might compare Russia's government with America's. Sometimes teachers in subjects other than English use the terms com-pare and contrast loosely: they may ask you to compare two things when they really mean compare and contrast. If a teacher in a subject like history asks you to "compare" two things, find out whether the teacher really wants you to just describe similarities, or whether descriptions of both similarities and differences are expected.

Once you are sure of the assignment, the first step is to make a table listing the similarities and/or differences for the two things. Such a table was shown for Superman versus Bond in the introduction, and for dogs versus cats in set 3. Starting with a table helps bring ideas to mind and organizes the ideas to form the basis for an effective paper. If you find you have listed more points in the table than you want to write about, select just those that you or your audience (e.g., teacher, employer, magazine subscribers) consider most important.

Your next step is deciding whether to employ the point-by-point or block-by-block pattern. For lengthier, more complicated topics the point-by-point pattern is easier to use. It allows you to deal with each point separately.

When you use the block-by-block pattern, you write about one thing completely and then the other. But as you write about the second thing, you must constantly refer back to the first one so your reader will think of both things together. For example, in the block-by-block paper on dogs versus cats, one sentence in the middle of the second block (cats) brought dogs back to mind by beginning, "As opposed to the silly antics and noisiness of dogs, a cat is . . ."

Another way of tieing the two blocks together is by using parallel structure, discussing the points in the same order within each block. In the dogs versus cats block-by-block paper the dog was first described in terms of personal needs, then noise, and finally companionship. In the second block, the cat was described on the same points in exactly the same order, so the differences between the two pets would be easy to see. If you don't use such techniques to unite the two blocks, it may seem like you are writing two separate essays.

Whichever pattern you select, certain words and phrases alert your reader to when you are discussing similarities, whereas others signal differences. Notice how "by contrast" and "but" are used in these examples to signal contrast.

A dog is always eager to please its master and will learn new tricks like "roll over" and "get the paper." BY CONTRAST, if you try to teach the same tricks to a cat, it becomes very impatient and sneaks away as soon as possible.

When you scold a dog, it hangs its head and with sad eyes begs for forgiveness. BUT if you scold a cat, it decides you aren't pleasant company and leaves until you change your attitude.

Here are some commonly used words and phrases for introducing comparisons and contrasts.

Words And Phrases For Introducing Similarities (Comparison)

both	Both movies and books . . .
similar to	Books are similar to movies . . .
also	Dogs also require . . .
like	Like dogs, cats must . . .
as well as	Dogs as well as cats offer . . .
resembles	Carob resembles chocolate in . . .
in common with	In common with movies, books provide . . .

others: just as, in the same way, in like manner, similarly, likewise

Words And Phrases For Introducing Differences (Contrast)

unlike	Unlike dogs, cats are . . .
another difference between	Another difference between European and Japanese cars . . .
in contrast to	In contrast to the fuel economy of small cars . . .
whereas	Whereas a dog . . .
in comparison to	In comparison to Shakespeare's comedies, those of Mel Brooks . . .
while	While books require reading skill, movies . . .

others: as opposed to, are different than, differ from, are dissimilar, however, but, larger than (faster than, etc.)

To begin a comparison/contrast paper you may introduce the topic by presenting a little background information and arousing the reader's interest. However, when you are pressed for time, as with essay exams, you may start simply by describing one of the similarities or differences for the two things you are writing about.

To close the paper, you could just finish with the final comparison or contrast. But often you will write a separate sentence or paragraph to summarize the ideas you have presented. Furthermore, if you prefer one thing or feel it is better than the other, you might express this opinion in your conclusion. Of course, the opinion you express should be supported and illustrated by the remainder of the paper. Examples of papers that end with an opinion are the McDonald's versus Arby's and the books versus movies selections.

In writing the main body of a comparison/contrast paper, remember to draw upon the writing skills and techniques you developed in earlier chapters. Most important, don't just make general statements; support and illustrate them by describing specific details. For example, in contrasting cars with motorcycles, don't just say cars are more comfortable. Describe the comforts: A car is enclosed so you are sheltered from rain and wind. It has a heater to keep you warm in the winter and an air conditioner for the summer. Supporting your ideas with details is just as important in a comparison/contrast paper as in a generalization–specifics paper.

Finally, the basic comparison/contrast paper can take many forms. For instance, in making a choice between two things—two typewriters or two restaurants—the differences between them often are more important than the similarities. A paper written for such a situation might have just one paragraph on similarities and then several paragraphs describing differences. Moreover, in a point-by-point paper, you don't always have to use exactly one paragraph for each point. If two points are closely related, you might deal with them both in a single paragraph. Or if a point is important and lengthy, you might use two or more paragraphs to explain and illustrate it fully. You can adopt the comparison/contrast pattern to fit the topic and purpose of the paper you are writing.

Independent Writing

1. Write a paper comparing and contrasting two of your friends. You may begin by creating a table like the one for James Bond and Superman. Your table should compare/contrast the physical characteristics as well as the personal qualities that make each a friend. Decide before you write if you want to use the point-by-point or block-by-block format. Also make sure that your characteristics are balanced (if you write about the athletic ability of one friend, write about the athletic ability of the other friend).

2. Write a paper (minimum 250 words) comparing and contrasting two cities (or a city vs. a town) which you have lived in, visited, or would like to see. Begin by making a table of similarities and differences. If you have trouble getting started, make a list of all the places you have been in the last year or the last 10 years. Then brainstorm and write down everything you remember doing or experiencing in these places.

3. Write a paper (minimum 250 words) on one of the following topics. Begin with a table listing similarities and differences.

   a. Compare and contrast a car with a house trailer (RV) as methods for traveling from New York to Los Angeles.
   b. Compare and contrast a plane with a train as methods for traveling from New York to Los Angeles.

Unit

11

Definition

To communicate precisely you sometimes need to define a word or term. The simplest type of definition is a synonym (a word having a similar meaning). For example, you could define the word "bizarre" by saying it means roughly the same as "strange." In defining a word this way, remember to use a synonym that is more familiar to your reader than the word you are defining. If a reader does not know what a "tumor" is, it probably will not help to write that a tumor is a "neoplasm."

Sometimes you cannot define a word with just a synonym because none exists. For instance, the word "synonym" does not have a synonym. To define "synonym" you must use a phrase like "a word having a similar meaning to another word." The word "carburetor" is another example. It has no synonym, but it can be defined by describing it with a sentence (sentence definition) such as this: A carburetor is a device on a gasoline engine used to blend and vaporize fuel and air.

Technical terms or words having personal significance (e.g., love, friendship) may require one or more paragraphs to fully explain their meaning. This is called an extended definition. For example, acid rain is mentioned in the news often. But what exactly is acid rain? An extended definition of this somewhat technical term might describe its chemical make-up, its origin, and its effect on the environment.

Turning from technical terms to personal ones with psychological impact, what do you mean by friendship? An extended definition of friendship might say friendship exists when people have common interests, show a willingness to help each other, and feel relaxed in each other's company. Each of these three expressions of friendship could be explained (and illustrated with examples) in separate paragraphs. The entire extended definition would form a paper of three or more paragraphs. The exercises in this unit illustrate extended definition papers.

Writing For Learning

Many of the following exercises ask you to write sentences in the best logical order. To obtain the greatest benefit, do not copy the words letter-by-letter. Instead, use these steps for each sentence.

1. Read as many words as you believe you can write correctly from memory (usually five to 10 words).

2. Write those words from memory, including all capitals and punctuation marks.

3. Check back to the original sentence and correct any errors you made.

4. Read the next group of words and repeat the above steps.

Generally you will be able to read, memorize, and correctly write between five and 10 words. Sometimes you may be able to remember an entire simple sentence correctly. But with a large, difficult-to-spell word, you may only try to write that one word correctly from memory. Writing from memory will make you more aware of the spelling, grammar, punctuation, and word patterns used in standard written English.

SET 1. FOOTBALL FANATIC

If you describe someone as a "safe driver" or a "football fanatic," you might explain what you mean by presenting several examples to illustrate the person's safe driving or football fanaticism. This is shown in the following exercises.

Exercise 1. Number the following sentences to form a paragraph describing a football fanatic.

> Vocabulary
> fanatic: person who is overly enthusiastic about something.
> plead: beg, request earnestly.

_____ He stares at football on the tube whether college or professional teams are playing.

_____ He doesn't care if it's the American, National, US, or Canadian league.

_____ He is a TV football fan-atic.

_____ My dad isn't a football fan.

_____ He spends all Saturday afternoon, Sunday afternoon, Monday and Tuesday evenings, and New Year's Day glued to the gridiron screen.

_____ He is certainly never moved by the pleadings of other family members for conversation, household help, or a change in TV programs.

_____ Sometimes the rest of us wish football had never been invented.

_____ An occasional trip to the kitchen or bathroom is all that moves him.

Exercise 2. Write the sentences in the order you numbered them to form a paper about a TV football fanatic.

Exercise 3. Write a paper about another type of fanatic—music, food, exercise, etc. Include details and, if possible, write about a person you know. For instance, if you write that your sister is a food fanatic, tell what she eats, when, how much, what food she dreams about, etc.

SET 2. THAT RAIN IS NOT WELCOME

What exactly is acid rain? The following sentences can be arranged into two paragraphs that define acid rain in terms of its composition, origin, and effects.

Exercise 1. For the first paragraph, number the sentences in the best logical order. For the second paragraph, order the destructive effects of acid rain from least to most important in your judgment. Conclude with a sentence about the future.

> Vocabulary
> pollutant: something that pollutes (makes dirty).

I

_____ These gases rise into the air, are chemically changed by sunlight, and mix with the moisture in clouds to form sulfuric and nitric acids.

_____ Factories, refineries, and power plants, especially those burning high-sulfur coal, give out smoke that is thick with sulfur dioxide gas.

_____ The clouds may travel hundreds of miles from the original source of pollution, but wherever they produce rain, acid is sprayed down from the sky.

_____ Its main cause is air pollution.

_____ Acid rain, a major environmental problem, is rain containing sulfuric and nitric acids.

_____ Automobile exhaust fumes are the primary source of another pollutant, nitrogen gas.

II

_____ In humans it damages the liver, lungs, and nervous system, and it also causes cancer.

_____ It eats away marble statues and stone buildings, and destroys forests and farm crops.

_____ If the human race is to remain alive and healthy into the 21st century, the causes of acid rain must be eliminated so that pure rain will again fall onto the earth.

_____ Acid rain is highly destructive.

_____ It kills entire populations of fish in lakes and rivers, causing million dollar losses to fishing and tourist industries, as well as threatening the existence of some fish species.

Exercise 2. Write the sentences in the order you numbered them to form a two-paragraph extended definition of acid rain.

SET 3. PHYSICAL FITNESS

Are you really "physically fit"? Find out by doing the following exercises.

Exercise 1. Number the sentences in each paragraph to form the best logical order.

I

_____ Experts say there are three components to physical fitness: cardiovascular fitness, muscular strength and endurance, and flexibility.

_____ Does playing baseball on weekends or going dancing several nights a week guarantee that you are physically fit?

_____ What is physical fitness?

II

_____ You will need a sturdy box or step that is 12 inches high.

_____ This component of fitness is important for living a healthy, long life.

_____ Cardiovascular fitness refers to the ability of the heart, lungs, and blood vessels to deliver blood and oxygen throughout the body.

_____ You can assess your cardiovascular fitness with a simple procedure called the Step Test.

_____ Now step down with your right foot and then your left foot.

_____ Step up with your right foot, then bring up your left foot.

_____ In fact, a well-conditioned college athlete generally has a Step Test pulse of less than 85.

_____ Go through this cycle 24 times a minute for 3 minutes.

_____ One final word of caution: If you have a heart condition, consult your physician before taking the Step Test.

_____ If your pulse rate is greater than 105 beats per minute, you could probably benefit from some cardiovascular conditioning exercise such as jogging, swimming, or cycling.

_____ Then wait 5 seconds and take your pulse for 1 minute.

III

_____ Your muscular strength differs from one body part to another, but abdominal strength is very important because these muscles help hold your internal organs in place and protect them from injury.

_____ This refers to the ability of the muscles in your legs, arms, chest, and abdominal (stomach) area to exert force for a period of time.

_____ To test your abdominal strength, see how many bent-leg sit-ups you can do.

_____ The second component of fitness is muscular strength and endurance.

_____ (Never perform straight-leg sit-ups because they can injure your back.)

_____ Roll up (don't jerk) until your elbows touch your knees, then return to the starting position.

_____ If you can't do 30 sit-ups, practice them about 5 days per week until your abdominal muscles meet this mark.

_____ Lie down with your legs bent to form a right angle at the knees and place your hands behind your head.

IV

_____ For example, if you lack lower back flexibility, you are more likely to hurt your back bending over to lift something.

_____ Slowly reach forward as far as you can.

_____ To test your lower back flexibility, sit on the floor with your legs together and straight.

_____ The final component of fitness, flexibility, concerns your ability to bend and stretch parts of your body fully.

_____ If you can't, you might consider starting a program of stretching exercises to increase your flexibility.

_____ Flexibility is important in avoiding muscle and joint injuries.

_____ Consider yourself flexible if you can reach 5 inches beyond your toes.

V

_____ However, a sports physician or physical education instructor can provide a more thorough evaluation of your overall fitness, and can recommend an exercise program to improve and maintain your fitness for life.

_____ The tests just described illustrate the three components of fitness.

Exercise 2. Write the sentences in the order you numbered them to form an extended definition of physical fitness.

Exercise 3. Based on exercise 2 or your own experience, make a paragraph-by-paragraph outline of facts for an extended definition paper on physical fitness. Limit your outline to a total of 100 words. Then put all other material away and write the paper (minimum 300 words) from the outline. Remember to read your first draft critically, correct spelling or grammar errors, and revise any sentences that can be rewritten to sound better or express ideas more clearly.

SET 4. STEPPARENT BLUES

What associations does the word stepparent bring to mind? Do you think of a mean, selfish person like Cinderella's stepmother? Here is the meaning of "stepparent" for a writer who is a stepparent.

Exercise 1. Number the sentences within each paragraph to form the best logical order.

Vocabulary
acquire: get, obtain.
advocate: a person who argues for the wishes of another.
co-conspirator: one who aids in an unlawful plan.
connotations: feelings and associations suggested by a word.
ego: self-pride, self-esteem.
ogre: monster, horrible giant that eats humans.
suspect (used as an adjective): open to suspicion.
reminiscing: thinking or talking about the past.
superficial: dealing only with the surface, shallow, lacking deep
         understanding.
tabloid: small size newspaper often with much sensationalistic
         news and gossip.
whims: sudden wishes or desires.

I

_____ It simply describes a stepparent as "the person who has married one's parent after the death or divorce of the other parent."

_____ Webster's gives a rather superficial definition of the word "stepparent."

_____ However, most stepparents have had experiences that give a much broader meaning to the word.

_____ This definition makes it seem easy to be a stepparent.

II

_____ But the word still sounds ugly and carries mean connotations.

_____ Today, as the divorce rate soars, the stepparent is becoming a common member of the family unit.

__3__ For centuries, stepparents have received more than their fair share of unkind press.

_____ In fact, due to these and other stories, stepmothers have become so suspect that many tales made up by children contain a "wicked stepmother" who terrorizes everyone in the fantasy.

_____ After all, wasn't it Cinderella's stepmother who almost worked the poor child to death?

_____ And wasn't Snow White's stepmother so jealous that she tried to kill the little princess?

__7__ Stepfathers haven't fared much better.

_____ Mr. Murdstone in _David Copperfield_ proved to be about as cruel as a stepfather could be.

_____ And tabloids have spread the news of stepfathers who have abused, molested, and murdered their stepchildren.

_____ In _Hamlet_, it was his stepfather who tried to murder the Danish prince.

III

_____ Now I hear protests of, "You don't know my stepmother (or stepfather)!" from some of you, and I admit you are right.

_____ Although in reality some stepparents are wicked and abusive, many more are nothing but good and kind to their stepchildren.

_____ But if the majority of you are honest, you will have to admit that your stepparent really isn't an ogre waiting for the chance to ruin your life forever.

_____ I don't know your stepparent, and he or she may be terrible.

IV

_____ And through the games of ego versus ego versus id, I have learned well the roles I am expected to play.

_____ The experiences that I've had are like a mixture of homemade sweet and sour sauce; even now I never know just what the "taste" of any situation is going to be.

_____ Putting all the fantastic tales and dictionary definitions aside, I believe I know what a stepparent really is because for 5 years I've known the burdens and the joys that accompany the title.

V

_____ I have also learned how to act at my husband's family gatherings when the <u>other</u> grandparents drop in and stay for hours reminiscing about the happy times when "the children" were married.

_____ As a stepparent I have learned to play the role of the cause for the breakup of my husband's first marriage and the disruptive effects it had on my stepchild, even though the marriage ended long before my husband and I met.

VI

_____ And early in my marriage I learned how to play the one who stayed at home when an outing suddenly became a "twosome."

__2__ Then I was expected to be the "absentee" when they could be present.

_____ Another role I learned was that of the "attendee" (my word) at school plays, dance recitals, and music extravaganzas when the real parents couldn't be there.

_____ But the most hurtful part I learned to play was how to watch my stepchild give good night kisses to everyone in the room — except me.

VII

_____ And more than once I have been a protector when tasks went undone or standards were not met.

___2___ Also, I have been the advocate when whiney whims became angry demands that soon turned to pitiful cries.

_____ Some of the sweeter times have occurred when my role required me to become a co-conspirator in helping acquire some wanted treasure, such as roller skates, a bicycle, or a computer.

_____ But these feelings lasted only until it was time for the child to visit the other parent, and he rushed off without remembering to say good-bye.

_____ During those times I said to myself, "I am the only person in the world who really understands this child."

VIII

_____ Who knows, maybe I'll even be invited to the wedding.

_____ Sometimes I think I do it just to find out if the good times will ever catch up with the bad ones.

_____ It is not easy to ride the emotional seesaw of stepparenthood day after day.

Exercise 2. Write the sentences in the order you numbered them to form an extended definition paper for "stepparent."

Analysis Of Extended Definition Papers

This unit has been placed last in the text because writing an extended definition generally taps a variety of the writing skills already covered. In writing extended definitions for "football fanatic," "acid rain," "physical fitness," and "stepparent," people and situations were described, cause–effect relationships were explained, sequences of actions were recounted, and examples were presented to illustrate general ideas. In this sense, writing extended definitions draws on all the writing skills practiced earlier.

The "Stepparent" paper highlighted an important distinction made regarding words that have personal or emotional meaning. The paper distinguished between the <u>denotative</u> meaning of "stepparent" and the <u>connotative</u> meaning to the writer.

The denotative meaning of a word is the definition that you find in the dictionary; it is basically the same for everyone. "Stepparent," for instance, has the following denotative meaning: the person who has married one's parent after the death or divorce of the other parent.

The connotative meaning of a word includes the feelings it suggests. For example, a person's "home" is more than just a building for shelter from the weather. "Home" has associated feelings that can produce "homesickness" when you are away from "home sweet home." These feelings form the connotative meaning of "home." The connotative meaning of a word is not the same for everyone because people's experiences differ. The "Stepparent" paper presented the connotative meaning of "stepparent" for the writer, herself a stepparent. A connotative meaning paper allows a writer to communicate personal feelings, helping people understand each other and themselves better. A stepchild (or the spouse of a stepparent) might develop greater sensitivity in family situations after reading the "Stepparent" paper. And another stepparent with similar frustrations could obtain comfort from reading the paper and realizing that he or she is not alone with these experiences. If an extended definition paper that you write brings greater insight and sensitivity to others, you have achieved a primary goal of writing.

Independent Writing

1. Write an extended definition of some term that is meaningful to you. Contrast the denotative and connotative definitions of the term to help the reader understand your perspective, as was done in "Stepparent Blues."

2. Your instructor may assign additional papers.

Beyond This Book: Combine Patterns To Fit Your Purpose

The units you have just completed illustrate some major patterns of thinking and writing. But you probably noticed that the pattern presented in each unit was frequently used in the papers of other units as well. For example, the cheese classification paper (unit 6) and the McDonald's vs Arby's comparison/contrast paper (unit 10) both included descriptions of how things looked and tasted (unit 2). The cheese paper described the cheese-making process and the steel drums paper described drum tuning, although process papers are the focus of unit 4. And the wheat kernel paper of unit 2 drew a *comparison* to an egg as a visual aid. In fact, classification papers almost always include statements on *comparisons* of objects in different categories, while comparison/contrast papers generally *classify* characteristics as "similar" and "different," and then further classify them into categories like—in dogs vs cats—*personal needs*, *noise*, and *companionship*.

In your own writing, combine the patterns in any way that allows you to best communicate your ideas. In a paper about commercial passenger planes you might begin with a physical description of a typical Delta jet, then recount the history of passenger planes, next describe some activities and operations—such as boarding, taking off, eating—and finally present some statistics and examples showing the importance of passenger planes in today's world. Several of the extended definition papers show other examples of how patterns can be combined. For instance, the Physical Fitness paper has the overall organization of a classification paper (three categories of fitness), but within each category there is a short *instructions* paper explaining how you can evaluate yourself on that component of fitness.

The patterned exercises in this book have strengthened your abilities to analyze relations and express ideas in standard written English. But as the above examples show, writing patterns can be combined in different ways to fit different topics. The only general pattern to use in writing almost any paper is to state your main points clearly, support and illustrate them with concrete examples and descriptions, and be willing to rewrite your paper several times as, each time you reread the paper, you find better ways to communicate your thoughts.

A Basic Glossary of Grammatical Terms and Punctuation

An <u>absolute phrase</u> is a noun + a participle that modifies an entire clause:

> The horse sailed over the fence, *its legs stretching upward and outward until it seemed to fly.*

An <u>adjective</u> (one of the eight parts of speech) describes or modifies a noun or pronoun. It tells you what kind, how many, and which one.

    a. what kind—this is done when you describe someone or something by telling its size, color, or other characteristic:
> The test was <u>easy</u>.
> There was a <u>big</u> explosion.
> She had <u>beautiful</u>, <u>black</u> hair.

    b. how many—tells just that:
> I always have a <u>few</u> cups of coffee during the day.
> I bought <u>six</u> doughnuts.
> She saw <u>many</u> of the stars of the show at the party.

c. which one — this can be done by using types of pronouns to describe a noun:

demonstrative

Pronoun ⟶	*Adjective*
This is mine.	This book is mine.
That was not funny.	That joke was not funny.
These are pretty.	These cups are pretty.
Those have to be washed.	Those socks have to be washed.

possessive

Pronoun ⟶	*Adjective*
His was lost.	His book was lost.
*Hers is gone.	*Her ruler is gone.
*Ours are missing.	*Our coats are missing.
*Theirs were eaten.	*Their cupcakes were eaten.
**Mine was thrown away.	**My paper was thrown away.
It's on the shelf.	Its place is on the shelf.
*Yours flew away.	*Your bird flew away.

*Notice that the -s is not used in the adjective forms of these pronouns.

**Notice that mine is changed to my when it is used as an adjective.

interrogative

Pronoun ⟶	*Adjective*
What is the answer?	What word will best describe Bryan?
Whose is this?	Whose sweater is on the floor?
Which is lost?	Which one of the lambs is lost?

(The interrogative pronouns also are relative pronouns that are not used to ask questions.)

indefinite

Pronoun ⟶	*Adjective*
Both are winners.	Both boys are winners.
None is left.	No milk is left.
Some are here.	Some friends are here.
Many went to the party.	Many celebrities went to the party.
Each is special.	Each friend is special.
Another has arrived.	Another relative has arrived.

There are three forms of adjectives used to show comparison:

positive — simple form —
    He is a <u>kind</u> person.

comparative — compares two —
    He is <u>kinder</u> than Louis.
    He is also <u>more intelligent</u> than Jon.

superlative — compares three or more —
    He is the <u>kindest</u> person in our class.
    He is the <u>most</u> intelligent person in our class.

SEE <u>Predicate Adjective</u>

An <u>adjective clause</u> is a clause that describes (modifies) a noun or pronoun. The entire clause acts as an adjective:

    The watch <u>that he wants</u> is too expensive.
              Adj. Clause

An <u>adjective phrase</u> is a phrase that describes (modifies) a noun or pronoun. The phrase is usually a prepositional phrase that acts as an adjective.

    I love the house <u>with the screened porch.</u>
              adj. phrase

An <u>adverb</u> (one of the eight parts of speech) describes (modifies) verbs, adjectives, or other adverbs. It tells how, when, where, why, how often, or to what degree:

    He came <u>here</u> <u>yesterday</u> and <u>quietly</u> purchased the <u>very</u>
          (where)(when)   (how)   (to what degree)

    expensive painting that he had <u>frequently</u> admired.
                  (how often)

Many adverbs are adjectivals (adjectives that are made adverbs by adding -ly to them):

    He has a <u>sharp</u> mind and tongue. (adjective)
    He spoke <u>sharply</u> to the waitress. (adverb)

Some words usually considered to be adjectives can be used as adverbs without changing the ending:

(adjective) He raised his <u>right</u> hand.
(adverb)   Turn <u>right</u> at the corner.

(adjective) The <u>early</u> bird catches the worm.
(adverb)   We arrived <u>early</u>.

An <u>adverb clause</u> is a subordinate clause that functions like a single adverb. It begins with a subordinating conjunction such as because, when, before, after, if, since, whether, although, while, where.

  *An adverbial clause must be part of a complete sentence. It never stands alone.

  *The subject of the adverbial clause will never be the subject of the sentence.

  *When an adverbial clause comes at the beginning of the sentence, it is usually followed by a comma.

  *When an adverbial clause comes at the end of the sentence, it is seldom preceded by a comma.

An <u>adverbial conjunction</u> is used to show the relationship between two independent clauses. The adverbial conjunction usually begins the second independent clause, but it may come within the second clause. If it begins the second independent clause, the adverbial conjunction is preceded by a seimcolon (;) and followed by a comma (,). If the adverbial conjunction comes within the second clause, the two clauses are still separated by the semicolon with the adverbial conjunction set off by commas.

Some common adverbial conjunctions include however, therefore, on the other hand, frankly, in fact, indeed, finally, consequently, furthermore, still, accordingly, thus.

  Jeff is the best basketball player on his team; in fact, he is the best player in the league.

  Judy is an excellent chess player; Nolan, however, is even better.

Writers often separate the two independent clauses with a period but still use the adverbial conjunction to begin the second sentence.

  Bonnie knew she had to get a good grade on the test in order to win the scholarship. Therefore, she stayed home all weekend and studied.

Because adverbial conjunctions show a relationship between two independent clauses, it is useful to be aware of the relationship that some major adverbial conjunctions express:

as a result	but	in addition
as a result	however	in addition
consequently	nevertheless	moreover
therefore		furthermore
thus		also

Occasionally, an adverbial conjunction is used as an interrupter in a sentence. It is set off by commas when it does this.

> Larry Ewing, however, will try to save the lives of Brittany and Dale on <u>Another World</u>.

An <u>adverb phrase</u> is usually a prepositional phrase that functions as an adverb.

> The dog ran <u>across the street</u>.   (where)

An <u>antecedent</u> is the noun to which a pronoun refers.

> Adam lost Adam's sweater, and Stephanie found Adam's sweater with Stephanie's book.

> Adam lost <u>his</u> sweater, and Stephanie found <u>it</u> with <u>her</u> book.

pronoun	antecedent
his	Adam's
it	Adam's sweater
her	Stephanie's

<u>Remember</u>

that two or more nouns (antecedents) joined by <u>and</u> are considered plural, and the pronoun must be plural;

> <u>Amanda and Sandy</u> want <u>their</u> breakfasts.

that if two or more singular nouns (antecedents) are joined by <u>or</u> or <u>nor</u>, the pronoun will be singular;

> <u>Amanda or Sandy</u> wants <u>her</u> breakfast.

that if two or more nouns (antecedents) joined by <u>or</u> or <u>nor</u> do not agree in number (one is singular; one is plural), the noun closest to the pronoun will determine the number of that pronoun;

Adam or the <u>boys</u> took <u>their</u> toys home.

The boys or <u>Adam</u> took <u>his</u> toys home.

that the indefinite pronouns anyone, everybody, everyone, each, neither, nothing, or anybody are singular and will require a singular pronoun.

<u>Everyone</u> wants <u>his</u> chance to win in the game of life.

Selecting the correct pronoun for the noun (antecedent) is a common task on many standardized tests. You may be asked to choose the correct pronoun or to find a pronoun that has been incorrectly used. If you remember that the pronoun must agree (be the same) in number (singular or plural) and gender (masculine or feminine or neuter) as you answer the question, the task will be easier for you.

An <u>apostrophe</u> (') is used to show ownership (-'s or -s'), to form contractions, and to make the plural forms of letters, numbers, and short words.

That is John<u>'s</u> shirt. (ownership)

He <u>doesn't</u> waste money; <u>I'm</u> sure of that! (contractions)

We need two <u>A's</u> for our poster.

<u>There are</u> no <u>and's</u>, <u>if's</u>, or <u>but's</u> about it!

When plural words end in -s, their possessive forms are made by adding the apostrophe after the -s:

dogs'   horses'   birds'   books'   sisters'

To indicate joint possession of something, add the -'s only to the last name:

Jon and Don's mother baked them special cakes every week.

A possessive is used when a gerund serving as a subject or object is preceded by a noun or pronoun:

Bryan's writing was greatly improved.

His sailing around the world began in October.

To indicate possession of something by a hyphenated word, place the -'s on the last part of the word:

My brother-in-law's father is rich.

To make a hyphenated word plural, the -s is added to the first word:

My brothers-in-law's fathers are rich.

This sentence means that I have more than one brother-in-law and that all of their fathers are rich.

An <u>appositive</u> is a noun, noun phrase, adjective phrase, or verb phrase that names, specifically identifies, or modifies another noun. It always comes immediately after the noun it is identifying.

When an appositive is necessary to the identification of the noun, it is considered <u>essential</u> and is <u>not</u> set off by commas. When an appositive just further describes or gives additional facts about the noun, then it is considered <u>nonessential</u> and <u>is</u> set off by commas:

Noun: Brenda, my sister, is an excellent typist.

Toby the elephant is the star of the circus.

Noun phrase:

Hemophilia, a hereditary condition in which one of the blood-clotting agents is missing, occurs in males.

Adjective phrase:

The boy skiing on one foot is my brother.

The new waitress, trying so hard to please everyone, fainted when she learned that she had delivered the wrong dinners to three different tables.

Verb phrase:

Jason's dream—to travel around the world—is about to begin.

(Using dashes instead of commas is usually more effective with verb phrases that are used in this way.)

When a name or title follows a phrase such as the movie, the writer, my sister, the novel, the short story, etc., it is considered essential and is not set off by commas:

My sister Brenda is an excellent typist.

The movie <u>The Raiders of the Lost Ark</u> was one of the most popular films of the year.

<u>Capitalization</u> has several rules that determine the use of capital letters. Use a capital letter.

a. to begin a sentence: The dog is a mutt.

b. to begin direct quotations: "It's good to be alive," she said.

c. for naming specific people: John, Lulu, Mother (<u>my</u> mother — when a possessive pronoun is used before mother, father, grandmother, etc., a capital letter is not used).

d. for naming specific places: Atlantic Ocean, Dover Street, St. John's River, a river, a street.

e. for naming areas of the country: I live in the <u>South</u>.

f. for naming specific historical events and documents:
the Civil War
the Declaration of Independence

("the" is not capitalized with the event or document unless it begins the sentence).

g. for naming titles of books (capitalize and underline)
<u>Little Women</u>   <u>Gone With the Wind</u>
<u>Black Boy</u>   <u>The Learning Tree</u>

h. for listing specific academic course:
American History 101   American history
Philosophy 200   philosophy

I usually hate political science, but Political Science 300 was a fantastic course.

i. for the days, months, and holidays: Tuesday, June, Thanksgiving (seasons of the year are not capitalized: fall, winter).

j. for any word that has to do with a race of people or a nationality: English, Spanish, Danish pastry, German chocolate cake.

k. to name specific groups, institutions, and businesses: Boy Scouts, Paintsville High School, Blackburn's Nursery.

l.   for specific religions, members of religious groups, and religious writings: Christianity, Baptists, Bible, Koran.

m. for the brand name of a product (but not the product): Zest soap, Ford truck, Wisk detergent.

*Small words (such as an, the, to, in, a) that appear in the middle of a title or name of specific person, place, thing, or artistic work are usually <u>not</u> capitalized.
<u>The Children of the Shell</u>
<u>Flowers in the Attic</u>

A <u>clause</u> is a group of words that has a subject and a verb. An independent clause expresses a complete thought:

The boy swam across the river.

A dependent clause does not express a complete thought; it begins with an introductory word that prevents the formation of a complete thought:

Even though it was raining very hard,

(This clause leaves the reader wondering about what happened next.)

Even though it was raining very hard, the ball game continued.

(This is a complete thought.)

See   Adjective Clause
Adverb Clause
Noun Clause

A <u>colon</u> (:) has several rules for its use:

Use a colon

a. before listing items following a complete sentence:
I have three favorite foods: chocolate pie, chocolate cake, and chocolate ice cream.

I enjoy eating the following foods: cookies, cake, and candy.

*Do not use a colon that separates a list from a preposition:

(Wrong) I like to: ride horses, swim, and read.
(Right) I like to ride horses, swim, and read.

b. between two closely related sentences for emphasis:
   Those caught stealing during the Middle Ages faced a stiff sentence: They were hung.

c. between a statement and an example of that statement:
   Use a capital letter to begin a sentence: The dog ran.

d. before a long quotation:
   The words of Thomas Carlyle are not just for teachers; they are for everyone: "That there should be one man (to) die ignorant who had the capacity for knowledge, this I call a tragedy."

e. after the salutation of a business or formal letter:
   Dear Madam:
   Dear Sir:
   To Whom It May Concern:
   Gentlemen:

f. between hours and minutes in time: 4:15 a.m., 11:40 p.m.

g. between Bible chapters and verses:
   My favorite Bible verses are John 13:34, 35.

h. between words that rhyme or show relationships of grammar:
   may:day
   blow:blew:blown

Coordinating Conjunctions link words, phrases, or clauses with grammatical equality. The coordinating conjunctions are and, but, for, or, nor, so, yet.

I like running, swimming, and reading.

The team won the game but lost the tournament.

A comma (,) is the most used (and misused) punctuation mark for separating ideas within a sentence. Although a pause is an indicator that a comma is needed, there are specific rules that must be observed when a comma is used.

Use a comma

a. to separate a series of three words or phrases:
   I love cookies, cake, and candy.

b. before the coordinating conjunction to separate two independent clauses:
   Mary will not eat meat, but she will eat eggs and drink milk.

c. after an introductory clause or phrase:
   Even though it was late, we went for a walk.

d. to separate two or more adjectives that modify the same noun:
Sharon wore a beautiful, long, blue dress.

e. to separate a direct quotation from its speaker:
Dan said, "I wish you would hire a tax consultant."
"I wish you would hire a tax consultant," Dan said.

*If the quoted sentence is a question or exclamation, the comma is not used if the quote is given before the identification of the speaker:
Dan asked, "Why don't you hire a tax consultant?"
"Why don't you hire a tax consultant?" Dan asked.

*Notice where the commas are placed when a quotation is split by the identification of the speaker:
"It is important to me," Mary sighed, "that you are a kind person."

(Be careful that you place the commas correctly in your sentences. And watch out for <u>one</u> of them to be omitted on a standardized test.)

f. to indicate parenthetical (nonessential) expressions:
The dog, however, was a beautiful animal.
The play, I assume, will begin on time.

g. to indicate the person to whom one is speaking in a direct address:
I think, John, that we should leave now.
Betty, will you come with us?

h. to separate a city from its state and the state from the rest of the sentence <u>if the two are used together</u>:
I lived in Paintsville, Kentucky, for 23 years.
He thinks Florida is the best state in the union.
You should visit Daytona Beach if you get the chance.

*Do not use a comma to separate a state from its zip code.
Daytona Beach, Florida 32018

i. to separate a street address from the city.
Mary lived at 711 North Street, Honolulu, Hawaii.

*If the street address is followed by a preposition, do not use a comma:
Mary lived at 711 North Street in Honolulu, Hawaii.

j. to separate an appositive or appositive phrase from the noun or pronoun it modifies:
I wish that Mrs. Jett, my second grade teacher, could see me now.

*If the appositive is closely related to its noun, a comma is not needed:

My sister Brenda is an excellent typist.

k. after the saluation and closing in an informal letter:

Dear Julie,   Sincerely,   Yours truly,

l. to improve the clarity of the sentence:

(unclear) Whenever Judy cooked Fred got sick.
(clear)   Whenever Judy cooked, Fred got sick.

m. to omit or repeat a word for effect:

Jim loved basketball; Ryan, baseball.
You may think you know everything, but it's love, love that really matters.

A comma splice occurs when two independent clauses are separated by a comma without using a coordinating conjunction.

(Wrong) I went home and studied, Judy went to the movies.

(Right) I went home and studied, but Judy went to the movies.

A complex sentence contains at least one dependent clause and one independent clause:

Even though it was dark, Nora went for a walk by the cliff.

A compound sentence has two or more independent clauses joined by a coordinating conjunction (preceded by a comma), or a semicolon, or a semicolon and a conjunctive adverb:

I thought the movie was excellent, but Tony thought it was terrible.

I liked the movie; Tony hated it.

I liked the movie; however, Tony hated it.

Conjunctions are words used to join related ideas. See adverbial conjunctions, coordinating conjunctions, and subordinating conjunctions.

Conjunctive adverbs are adverbial conjunctions. See adverbial conjunctions.

<u>Contractions</u> are formed when two words are joined by omitting certain letters and using an apostrophe to represent those letters:

Not becomes <u>n't</u>. It can be added only to these verbs to make the following contractions:

aren't	hadn't	needn't	wouldn't
can't	hasn't	oughtn't	
couldn't	haven't	shan't	
didn't	isn't	shouldn't	
doesn't	mightn't	wasn't	
don't	mustn't	won't	

The following verbs can be added to <u>pronouns</u> and <u>there</u> to make contractions:

is	becomes	's	he's	there's
are	becomes	're	they're	there 're
has	becomes	's	he's	there's
had	becomes	'd	he'd	there'd
would	becomes	'd	he'd	there'd
have	becomes	've	we've	there've
will	becomes	'll	she'll	there'll
am	becomes	'm	I'm	(am is used only with I)

Contractions are used in informal writing but are usually not accepted in formal writing (check with your instructor before using them in your essays).

A <u>declarative sentence</u> makes a statement. Elaine went to the store.

A <u>direct object</u> is the noun or pronoun that receives the action of the verb:

The quarterback threw the ball.
(subject)   (verb)   (d.o.)

The easiest way to determine the direct object is to find the verb (the verb must be an <u>action</u> verb before there can be a direct object): Ask yourself,

"What is the action of the sentence; what's someone or something doing, done, or going to do?"

Threw

Then determine the subject by asking yourself exactly who or what did the verb.

Who or What threw? <u>Quarterback</u> threw

Next, say the subject, verb, and "What or Whom":

Quarterback threw "What or Whom"

Quarterback threw ball
(sub)   (V)   (d.o.)
ball = direct object

Now do this sentence:

One of the girls petted all of the dogs.

1. What is the action; what happened? <u>petted</u> (verb)

2. Exactly who "petted"? <u>one</u> (subject—only one did the petting; <u>of the girls</u> is a prepositional phrase, so girls cannot be the subject.)

3. One petted "What or Whom?" <u>all</u> (direct object—of the dogs is a prepositional phrase, so dogs cannot be the subject.)

*The direct object can <u>never</u> be in a prepositional phrase.

*If the direct object is a pronoun, it will always be an objective case pronoun (me, him, her, us, them, whom, you, it)

See Indirect Objects

An <u>ellipsis</u> (. . .) is used to indicate that something has been omitted from a direct quotation. Many mistakes are made when ellipsis marks are used to substitute for colons, commas, or dashes. An ellipsis can also be used at the end of a sentence to imply a trailing thought or action.

An <u>exclamatory sentence</u> expresses strong emotion or excitement. It ends with an exclamation mark (!).

A <u>gerund</u> is a present participle (verb + ing) used as a noun:

<u>Running</u> is my husband's favorite sport.

Because it functions as a noun, a gerund may be the subject of the sentence or dependent clause, the object of a preposition, the direct object, or the subject complement.

A gerund phrase includes all the words that are attached to the gerund and acts as a noun with the gerund:

Riding bicycles is a relaxing hobby.
(g.p. = subject)

My son loves swimming in the ocean
                              (g.p. = direct object)

His favorite pastime is lifting weights.
                              (g.p. = complement)

A hyphen (-) is a punctuation mark used

a. to indicate where a word is divided into syllables: doc-tor

b. to make certain compound words by combining two nouns or an adjective and a noun: a free-lance artist

c. between the root word and certain prefixes and suffixes: president-elect, semi-invalid, ex-wife, self-reliant

d. with numbers written out from twenty-one to ninety-nine: thirty-nine, fifty-six, eighty-seven

    When the number is greater than ninety-nine, the hyphen is used only between the parts of the number less than ninety-nine:
    sixty-five hundred (6500)   five hundred and forty-two (542)

    Fractions that are written out use a hyphen:
    two-fifths of a quart, one-third full

    A hyphen is used to indicate that everything between two numbers is included:
    1960–1965
    98–127

e. between the names of nations or people to create an adjective: Chino-Japanese War, Bryan-Chamorro Treaty

f. between a prefix and a specific noun (usually pertaining to a nation or group of people):
    anti-Latin America, pro-Egypt, ex-Marine

g. to separate a compound modifier that is used before a noun:
    He was the best-dressed man at the party.
    He was the best dressed.

    If one of the modifiers is an adverb ending in-ly, do not use the hyphen:
    Howard's truck had a finely tuned engine.

  h. when making a compound word that would have an awkward
     spelling: The herd was <u>bull-less</u>.

  i. for clarity within a sentence when the position of certain words
     may cause confusion: He was a <u>hard-drinking</u> man.

  j. to indicate that a word is spelled out or stuttered:
     "You must understand that <u>t-h-e-r-e</u> and <u>t-h-e-i-r</u> have differ-
     ent meanings," said the teacher.

     "<u>Wh-wh-what</u> is that?" Sean asked.

An <u>imperative sentence</u> makes a request or gives a command. It may
end with a period or exclamation mark. Sometimes the subject is
named in the sentence; sometimes the subject is <u>you understood</u>.

    John, be quiet!

    Please give me the book, Mary.

    Go away!

An <u>indirect object</u> comes before the direct object and expresses the
thought "<u>to</u> or <u>for</u> what or whom" the action of the verb occurred.

      I bought David a book.
     (s)   (v)   (i.o.)   (d.o.)

    *The easiest way to find the indirect object is to first find the verb,
     the subject, and the direct object. When you have found these, say
     them together and add "to or for what or whom."

    Mary baked Dan a cake.

    Verb: <u>baked</u>
    Subject: Who "baked" something? <u>Mary</u>
    Direct object: Mary baked "what or whom?" <u>cake</u>
    Indirect object: Mary baked cake "for what or whom?" <u>Dan</u>

Sometimes students make a mistake and call the indirect object the direct object. But if you realize that Mary baked a cake—she did not
bake <u>Dan</u>—it will be easier to find the indirect object.

    *The indirect object will always come <u>before</u> the direct object.

*If <u>to</u> or <u>for</u> precedes the noun or pronoun that answers the question of the indirect object, then you have the <u>object of a preposition</u> (there will be no indirect object):

Mary baked for Dan a cake.   (this structure is rarely used)
  (s)   (v)   (o.p.)   (d.o.)

Mary baked a cake for Dan.   (more common structure)
  (s)   (v)   (d.o.)   (o.p.)

John threw Ted the football.
  (s)   (v)   (i.o.)   (d.o.)

John threw the football to Ted.
  (s)   (v)   (d.o.)   (o.p.)

*If a pronoun is the indirect object, it will always be an <u>objective case pronoun</u>. See <u>objective case</u>.

An <u>infinitive</u> is <u>to + the base form of a verb</u>. It is used as a noun (as the subject, subject complement, or direct object) or as an adjective or adverb modifier: Jeff likes <u>to swim</u>.

An <u>infinitive phrase</u> is all the words that go with the infinitive. It is usually an infinitive + a prepositional phrase.

Jeff and Glenn just want <u>to swim across the lake</u>. (direct object)

His goal was <u>to run in the Boston Marathon</u>. (subject complement)

<u>To get home safely</u> was her only concern. (subject)

Theodore Roosevelt exercised <u>to improve his health</u>. (adverb)

Jessica is the girl <u>to beat</u>. (adjective)

An <u>interrogative sentence</u> asks a question and ends with a question mark: Do you think we will win?

An <u>intransitive verb</u> does not have a direct object or a subject complement.

Beth slept in the tent.

John ran.

A <u>linking verb</u> "links" the subject to its subject complement (predicate nominative or predicate adjective). It is sometimes called a "state of being" verb because it describes the condition of the subject or renames it.

The most common linking verbs are the forms of to be: is, are, was, were. But verbs that state conditions also are linking verbs:

feel, smell, taste, seem, appear, sound

He feels tired.

The pie tastes good.

The sea sounds rough.

Cheri is the winner.

A <u>noun</u> is the name of a person, place, thing, idea, or emotion. Although it is usually easy to identify the nouns that name people, places, and things, those nouns that refer to ideas or emotions often are missed by students. So remember that words such as happiness, peace, courage, heroism, love (my love), hatred, hate, and contentment are nouns.

*words that end in -ance, -ence, -tion, -sion, -or, -er, -ism, -ty, -ship, -ture, -ness, -ment are usually nouns.

A <u>noun clause</u> is a dependent clause that is used in a sentence as the subject, indirect object, direct object, predicate nominative, or the object of a preposition:

I hope <u>that he wins the race.</u> (direct object)

<u>Where she will go to school</u> is still a mystery. (subject)

The only regret of my youth <u>is that I never saw the Beatles on stage.</u> (predicate nominative)

<u>Number</u> refers to changes in words that indicate if a word is singular or plural:

That boy is a winner. (singular)

Those boys are winners. (plural)

The <u>objective</u> case is a noun or pronoun used as the direct object, indirect object, or object of the preposition.

*The following are objective <u>case</u> pronouns:

me, him, her, us, them, whom

These pronouns are used only in the objective case; none of them can be used as the subject or subject complement of a sentence.

You and it are both objective and subjective case pronouns and function as either case.

Parallelism is the repetitive use of words or phrases with the same grammatical structure. This is used to bind ideas by creating unity within a single sentence or between sentences.

He loves running, swimming, and riding.

Jim promised to take out the garbage, to make his bed, and to sweep his room.

Many standardized tests include questions that examine your ability to determine parallelism. You may be asked to read a group of sentences and select the one that is the most correct:

a. John liked swimming, biking, and to read.
b. John liked to swim, biking, and to read.
c. John liked swimming, biking, and reading.
d. John liked swimming, to bike, and to read.

Of the four sentences above, c is the most correct because the parallel structure is maintained in the -ing endings.

Watch out for parallelism on tests.

Watch out for parallelism in your essays.

A parenthetical expression is a nonessential phrase. See comma f.

A participle is a verb used as an adjective or an adverb.

A participle phrase consists of the present or past participle and any words used with it.

Swinging through the air, the trapeze artist was a portrait of confidence and grace.

The vase broken by the child could not be repaired.

A <u>past participle</u> is the third principle part of a verb:

		(past participle)
walk	walked	walked
grow	grew	grown
ride	rode	ridden

When the past participle is used as a verb, it must be used with an auxiliary verb:

We <u>had walked</u> by the pond many times.

The food <u>was grown</u> in our garden.

We <u>have ridden</u> all day.

When the past participle is used as an adjective, it does not need the auxiliary verb:

The <u>ridden</u> horses were tired.

The <u>broken</u> vase could not be repaired or replaced.

A <u>period</u> (.) is an end mark of punction. It is used to mark the end of a sentence that is a statement, a weak command, or an indirect question.

It is also used after abbreviations and initials:

Dr., Mr., Ms., Rev., James M. Blanton, Sr., Washington, D.C., Ky.

Many familiar groups of initials or acronyms do not use periods:

YMCA   NASA   tv   UN   USA

Most radio and television call letters do not use periods:

WKEE   WMMR   WKISS   CBS

A <u>phrase</u> is a group of words that are grammatically related but do not form a complete sentence.

A <u>predicate adjective</u> is an adjective that describes the subject of the sentence. It always follows a linking verb.

> Jim is <u>smart</u>.
>
> The pie smells <u>good</u>.
>
> (See <u>linking verb</u>)

A <u>predicate nominative</u> is a noun or pronoun that follows a linking verb and renames the subject of the sentence.

> Paul is the <u>winner</u>. (Winner renames the subject.)
>
> Eleanor is an intelligent <u>woman</u>.

If a pronoun is used, it must be a subjective case pronoun: I, he, she, we, they, you, who, it.

> It was <u>he</u> who hit the home run.

A <u>preposition</u> is a word used before its object (a noun and its modifiers, or a pronoun) to indicate its relation to another word in the sentence.

There are almost 100 words used as prepositions; these are some of the more common ones:

about	because of	but	into	over	underneath
above	before	by	like	past	until
across	behind	down	near	since	up
after	below	due to	next to	through	upon
against	beneath	except	off	till	with
among	beside	for	of	to	within
at	between	from	on	toward	without
away from	beyond	in	out	under	

A <u>prepositional phrase</u> includes the preposition and its noun (and modifiers) or pronoun. The prepositional phrase is used as an adjective or an adverb.

> The bread <u>in the plastic bag</u> is <u>for the hungry birds</u>.
>   (adjective)   (adjective)
>
> The ship sailed <u>with the wind and the tide</u>.
>   (adverb)

A <u>present participle</u> is the first principle part of a verb + -ing:

	(present participle)
talk	talking
sing	singing
play	playing

When the present participle is used as a verb, it is used with an auxiliary verb:

Rick <u>was talking</u> to Erin.

Laura and Bill <u>were playing</u> backgammon.

Bobby <u>is singing</u> in the shower.

When the present participle is used as an adjective or an adverb, it is not used with the auxiliary verb.

(adj.) The <u>running</u> boy frightened the birds.

(adv.) The thieves ran, <u>bumping into everyone</u>.

A <u>pronoun</u> is a word that takes the place of a noun. See <u>subjective case</u>, <u>objective case</u>, <u>possessive case</u> pronouns.

The <u>possessive</u> case expresses ownership. Singular possessive nouns are formed by adding <u>-'s</u>. The possessive case of regular plural nouns (those ending in <u>s</u> or <u>es</u>) is formed by adding an ':

	singular	plural
	dog's	dogs'
	Burgess's	Burgesses'
(or Burgess')		

An irregular noun that changes when it becomes plural is made possessive by adding an <u>'s</u>:

woman's	women's
mouse's	mice's

<u>Possessive case pronouns</u> (used as modifiers) include my, mine, his, her, hers, our, ours, their, theirs

Michael knows that is <u>his</u> baseball.

Jacquie is at <u>my</u> house.

The horse is <u>mine</u>.

That is <u>her</u> sweater.

That sweater is <u>hers</u>.

Possessive case pronouns do not use apostrophes.

<u>A question mark</u> (?) is used at the end of an interrogative (direct question) sentence:

How are you today?

An indirect question does not use a question mark:

Mary wondered if Brenda was going to the concert.

Jack wanted to know who they were.

(These sentences are statements about what Mary wondered and what Jack wanted. Neither actually asks a question.)

<u>Quotation marks</u> (" ") are used

a.   to indicate a direct quotation:

"I want to travel to faraway places," said Teri.
"The house is on fire!" screamed Mother.
"When will you be home?" asked Father.

Teri said, "I want to travel to faraway places."
Mother screamed, "The house is on fire!"
Andrea asked, "When will you be home?"

"Even if you don't love me, I love you," Joan sighed.

*Pay attention to the placement of punctuation marks used with the quotation marks. Look at them carefully. Notice where the commas, periods, question marks, and exclamation marks are placed in relationship to the quotation marks.

Many times a quotation may be interrupted by the identification of the speaker. The punctuation is different when it is.

"When my brother grows up," said Jason, "he wants to be a space traveler."

Notice that there is a comma before the quotation begins again. It comes <u>before</u> the second set of quotation marks, too.

Sometimes the split will occur between sentences of the quotation:

"I wonder who will be the next victim," she whispered. "It could be either one of us."

Notice that there is a period after whispered in this quotation.

b. to enclose titles of chapters of books, short stories, magazine articles, essays, short poems, one-act plays, works of art, and songs:

"Love Me Tender" is a beautiful song.

c. to call attention to words that have a special meaning within the sentence:

Let's "boogaloo" at a club tonight.

When a word or phrase is quoted within a quotation, it will be set off with a single quote:

Mary asked her students, "Can anyone spell 'genuine'?"

*Remember that you must have two double quotation marks for punctuating a regular quote; four will be used if the quotation is split. Standardized tests may omit one of the quotation marks or one of the punctuation marks preceding it. You must look for these errors on tests and within your essays.

A <u>semicolon</u> is used

a. to join two independent clauses without using a coordinating conjunction:

Jim is a thoughtful man; he treats each of his employees to lunch once a month.

b. to join two independent clauses using a conjunctive adverb:

Jane worked all day and was very tired when she got home; however, she stayed up half the night studying for a biology test.

    c. to join two independent clauses using a coordinating conjunction that is followed by a dependent clause:

> Maria loved Lewis very much; but because she had obligations to her blind mother, she would not marry him.

    d. to make clear the separation between items of a long list:

> The band consists of Mike, the pianist; John, the drummer; Tom, the guitarist, and Ben, the singer.

> Using the semicolon in this manner indicates that Mike <u>is</u> the pianist, that John <u>is</u> the drummer, that Tom <u>is</u> the guitarist, and that Ben <u>is</u> the singer. Without the semicolon, it would not be clear if Mike was the pianist, etc. The semicolon also makes it clear that there are four members in the band instead of eight that would be suggested if only commas were used.

A <u>sentence fragment</u> may seem to be a sentence; however, it lacks the necessary grammatical elements to make it a complete thought:

> (Fragment) Although it was a dark, stormy night.

This fragment begins with a capital letter, has a subject (it) and a verb (was) and even a complement (night), but the introductory <u>Although</u> is a subordinating conjunction and causes this to be a dependent clause that needs to be attached to an independent clause:

> (Sentence) Although it was a dark, stormy night, Troy went for a walk by the cliffs.

> (Fragment) <u>Of his love</u>. I am sure.

Of his love is a prepositional phrase; it does not have a subject or a verb.

> Of his love I am sure.

> I am sure of his love.

Both of these are sentences; both make a complete thought. Look at the next example.

> We walked home in the dark. <u>Because we missed the bus.</u>
>   (Sentence)   (Fragment)

When combined with the sentence, the fragment makes sense.

We walked home in the dark because we missed the bus.

*Watch for phrases (prepositional, participle, explanatory, appositive, or infinitive) and clauses (noun, adjective, or adverb) pretending to be sentences. Learn to spot them on tests as well as in your essays.

*With writing styles becoming less formal, more writers are using fragments for effect. If you want to use a fragment, make sure that it is effective and that your teacher knows you have used a fragment and approves of it.

Sentence patterns have developed over the centuries into five basic patterns:

Subject + verb
Subject + linking verb + subject complement
Subject + action verb + direct object
Subject + action verb + indirect object + direct object
Subject + action verb + direct object + object complement

A simple sentence expresses one complete thought and has only one independent clause:

The car stopped by my house.

The subjective case is used as the subject of the sentence and the subject complement (predicate nominative) that follows a linking verb. When a pronoun is used as the subject or subject complement, only subjective case pronouns can be used:

I   he   she   we   they   who   you   it

The subject complement comes after a linking verb and renames (noun or pronoun = predicate nominative) or modifies (predicate adjective) the subject.

See predicate nominative and predicate adjective

The verb used with subjects joined by <u>either/or</u> and <u>neither/nor</u> will be determined by the subject <u>nearest</u> the verb:

Either <u>Juan</u> or <u>Lewis</u> <u>is</u> the winner.
     (s)   (s) (s)

Either <u>they</u> or <u>Steven</u> <u>wins</u> the money.
     (p)   (s)   (s)

Either <u>John</u> or <u>they</u> <u>win</u> the contest.
     (s)   (p) (p)

Neither the <u>boys</u> nor the <u>girls</u> of this school <u>are going</u>.
        (p)   (p)   (p)

Collective nouns use a singular verb if the sentence refers to the group as a single unit. If the collective noun refers to all the individuals of the group, a plural verb is used.

The team is going to the Orange Bowl.

The team are learning their plays.

A verb following a relative pronoun (that, who, whom, which) that is used in a modifying clause must agree in number with the antecedent of the pronoun.

I like doctors who are concerned about their patients.

I like a doctor who is concerned about her patients.

A verb that is separated from the subject by a phrase which begins <u>in addition</u>, <u>along with</u>, <u>including</u>, <u>as well as</u>, <u>together with</u>, etc., is <u>not</u> changed because of the noun or pronoun in the phrase:

The <u>woman</u>, along with her children, <u>waits</u> here for the bus.

The two <u>boys</u>, along with Marcia, are going with us.

Sondra, as well as Clint, is coming for a visit.

Subject/verb agreement means that the subject and verb must be the same in number (singular or plural):

A singular subject must have a singular verb:

Mary sings; Charles sings.
She runs very fast.

A singular present-tense verb ends with -s.

A plural subject must have a plural verb:

Joanne and Glenn sing very well.
They sing in the church choir.

A plural verb does not end with -s.

When I is the subject, use a plural present-tense verb—except for are: Use I am, never I are:

I run every day.
I ride my bicycle twice a week.
I am an active person.

Be sure that you know the correct subject before you try to determine if the verb is singular or plural:

One of the girls _____ coming to my house.
              is/are

In the preceding sentence, one is the subject and is is the verb. Girls is in a prepositional phrase and cannot be the subject of the sentence.

When the sentence order is inverted, make sure you select the right subject:

There is only one thing that I have to say.

Quickly ran the rabbit away from the hunters.

A verb following an indefinite pronoun will be singular or plural depending on the number of the pronoun:

Singular	Plural	*Singular or Plural
anybody	both	all
everybody	few	any
nobody	many	most
somebody	several	none
anyone		some
everyone		more
no one		
someone		*Read the sentence carefully to
each		determine if the pronoun is singular or
either		plural:
many a		
neither		Most of the soup is gone.
one		(s) (s) (s)
anything		
everything		Most of the players are here.
nothing		(p) (p) (p)
something		

No one is going.
Anyone is capable of doing the job.
Someone was in this office last night.

Several of us are going to the movies.
A few are going to study.
Both eat too much.

The subjunctive mood of verbs is used to express contrary to fact, uncertain, or desired conditions. It also is used with certain subordinate "that" clauses:

I wish he were here so I could be happy.
If she were gone, we could go.
The parents' only hope is that their child be returned safely.

A <u>transitive verb</u> has a direct object (and sometimes an indirect object or an object complement).

> I hit John.
> (t.v.) (d.o.)
>
> Mary baked Dan a cake.
> (t.v.)   (i.o.)   (d.o.)
>
> The banker's attitude made him a ruthless man.
> (t.v.) (d.o.)   (o.c.)

The <u>tense</u> of a verb expresses time: present, past, and future.

The simple tense is formed in the following manner:

> Present— add -s to form 3rd person singular present tense; the plural form does not use the -s;
>
> Past—   add -ed to form the past tense of regular; an irregular verb has a different form;
>
> Future— add shall or will to the present tense plural (even for the 3rd person singular).

The perfect tense requires auxiliary verbs:

> present perfect tense—have or has + past participle
> past perfect tense—had + past participle
> future perfect tense—shall have or will have + past participle

The progressive tense requires a form of to be + present participle. See participle.

A <u>verb</u> expresses action or state-of-being (copulative) or links the subject to a subject complement. See also <u>intransitive</u>, <u>linking</u>, <u>and transitive verb</u>; <u>tense</u>.

Verbs have three principle parts:

	regular	irregular
present tense :	sip	go
past tense :	sipped	went
past participle:	sipped	gone

A <u>verbal</u> is a gerund, participle, or infinitive. It is used most commonly as a noun or adjective.

See gerund, participle, infinitive

A <u>verb phrase</u> is the verb or the verb and any helping verb occurring with it:

He <u>went</u> home.   He <u>was going</u> home.
    (vp)   (vp)

The <u>voice</u> of the transitive verb is either active or passive. The active voice means that the subject acts upon something. The passive voice indicates that something has acted upon the subject.

(Active)   The quarterback threw the football.

(Passive)   The football was thrown by the quarterback.

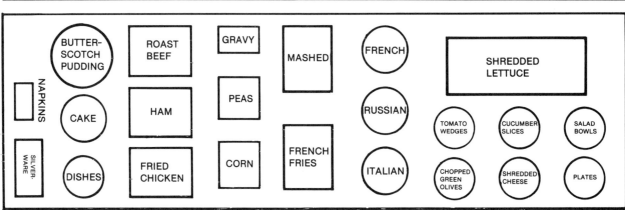